Julian Kennedy Smyth

Holy Names

As Interpretations of the Story of the Manger and the Cross

Julian Kennedy Smyth

Holy Names
As Interpretations of the Story of the Manger and the Cross

ISBN/EAN: 9783337280758

Printed in Europe, USA, Canada, Australia, Japan

Cover: Foto ©Lupo / pixelio.de

More available books at **www.hansebooks.com**

HOLY NAMES

HOLY NAMES.

✠

As Interpretations
of
The Story of the Manger
and the Cross.

✠

BY THE

REV. JULIAN K. SMYTH,

AUTHOR OF "FOOTPRINTS OF THE SAVIOUR."

He dwelleth with you, and shall be in you. — 2 JOHN XIV. 17.

BOSTON:
ROBERTS BROTHERS.
1891.

University Press:
JOHN WILSON AND SON, CAMBRIDGE, U.S.A.

To my Wife.

"God hides Himself within the love
Of those whom we love best;
The smiles and tones that make our homes
Are shrines by Him possessed."

PREFACE.

THE title of this little volume refers to that wonderful list of names applied to the Son of Man in the well-known prophecy: "Unto us a child is born; unto us a Son is given; and the government shall be upon His shoulder; and His name shall be called Wonderful, Counsellor, the Mighty God, the Everlasting Father, the Prince of Peace." The emotions experienced upon hearing Handel's mighty chorus, in which these holy names, one after the other, are proclaimed with such power, led the author to make a special study of these five titles. He felt then — and he feels more than ever now — that there is a power of meaning in them; that the appellations, as well as the order in which they are given, are not accidental. The result of these studies is the conviction that there is a beautiful and divinely-intended sequence of ideas in these names and titles; that they help to interpret for us the story of the manger and the cross by indicating the different ties and relationships which our Lord by His life on earth sought to establish; and that in a manner at once impressive and helpful they suggest — or, more properly speaking, they reveal — those spiritual relationships which one after another are intended to grow up between the Lord and every follower who is faithful unto the end. Each tie, each new bond formed, is of a more intimate and sacred character than the preceding, until from that first wonder, or admiration with which we regard Him, He becomes at last the peace-giver.

It is this spiritual side of the Christ-life as it touches and enters into our human life, the progressiveness of it, the helpfulness and the beauty of it, which this little book seeks most of all to express. In two of the earlier chapters, the author has not hesitated to enter with some degree of particularity into the subject of the virgin-birth, stating some principles which he trusts may prove helpful in thinking clearly of this great fact of incarnation. In the Appendix, he has endeavored to emphasize the historic truthfulness of the person of the Son of Man as revealed in the Gospels, and the divine character of His life and work. In a companion volume,[1] he has tried to make real to thought and affection the Humanity of our Lord. In these pages, and by means of these Holy Names, his main purpose has been to help such as may read this book to think of the Lord's inward presence as a most sacred reality, and a never-failing means of support and comfort.

However inadequately this purpose may have been fulfilled, this little book is now sent forth with "God-with-us" as its watchword, and this promise of the Gospel as its chief message: "He dwelleth with you, and shall be in you."

[1] Footprints of the Saviour.

BOSTON, October, 1891.

CONTENTS.

✠

	PAGE
THE HOLY NAMES	13
A Chapter for Christmas Day.	
I. THE LORD AS THE WONDERFUL . .	37
II. THE LORD AS THE COUNSELLOR . .	59
III. THE LORD AS THE MIGHTY GOD . .	81
IV. THE LORD AS THE EVERLASTING FATHER	105
V. THE LORD AS THE PRINCE OF PEACE .	131

Appendix.

A. THE STORY OF THE VIRGIN-BIRTH.—ITS AUTHENTICITY	161
B. A LAW OF CREATION AS APPLIED TO THE MIRACULOUS CONCEPTION	166
C. THE PERSON OF THE SON OF MAN IN THE LIGHT OF HIS OWN TESTIMONY .	170
D. A VENERABLE AND REMARKABLE WITNESS	176
E. THE SIMPLICITY OF THE GOSPEL-RECORDS, AND THE MIRACULOUS ELEMENT . .	185
F. THE STORY OF THE REDEMPTION . . .	189

THE HOLY NAMES.

O TENDER tale of old,
   Live in thy dear renown;
God's smile was in the dark, behold
   That way His hosts came down;
Light up, great God, thy Word;
   Make the blest meaning strong,
As if our ears, indeed, had heard
   The glory of their song.

It was so far away,
   But Thou could'st make it near,
And all its living might display
   And cry to it, "Be here,"—
Here, in th' unresting town,
   As once remote to them,
Who heard it when the heavens came down,
   On pastoral Bethlehem.

It was so long ago,
   But God can make it *now*,
And as with that sweet overflow,
   Our empty hearts endow;
Take, Lord, those words outworn,
   O! make them new for aye,
Speak — "Unto you a Child is born,"
   To-day — to-day — to-day.

Holy Songs, Carols, and Sacred Ballads.

The Holy Names.

A CHAPTER FOR CHRISTMAS DAY.

✣

" For unto us a Child is born: unto us a Son is given: and the government shall be upon His shoulder; and His Name shall be called Wonderful, Counsellor, the mighty God, the everlasting Father, the Prince of Peace."

MUCH of the joy which Christmas day should bring, is in feeling that this old fact of the Incarnation still lives; that it still is true; that it still holds the promise of the Divine nearness and loving-kindness. Can we ask more, can we do more than to read the story of the Nativity out of our Gospels; to try and bring this event before ourselves as distinctly as possible; to remember the love, of which it is a sign, the blessings, of which it is a source, and then to take the words of this ancient prophecy, and still keeping them in their present tense, say, as expressive of a present joy and a present comfort, "Unto us a Child is born; unto us a Son is given."

It was some seven hundred years and more prior to the Nativity that Isaiah uttered this prophecy. A long period; and yet by direction of Him to Whom "a thousand years are but as yesterday," the prophecy comes to us speaking in the present tense. More than eighteen hundred years are passed since the prophecy received its outward fulfilment in the city of David, more than twenty-five hundred years since it was first proclaimed in Jerusalem; and still, as we repeat it, we keep proclaiming the fact it holds as a present fact, the promise it offers as a present promise. A thousand years hence, Christian men and women will still be saying, "Unto us a Child is born; unto us a Son is given."

Now there is something extremely impressive in the Divine expectation thus disclosed, that men would find something ever fresh and gladdening in this fact of the Incarnation; that instead of being the close of a promise made years before, a settling up, as it were, of God's account with the Church, it would prove to be the sign and the means of new beginnings,—in the world's history, a beginning; and a beginning just as truly in the spiritual history of every true Christian follower. In other words, God, as the Psalmist has expressed it, is "a very *present* help in trouble." With Him it is now, to-day, if we will hear his voice; fresh help, fresh power. And I think we may safely say that, as an aid in thinking of the presence and the saving power of our Lord as perpetual, it was intended that we should say, "Unto us a Child *is* born; unto us a Son *is* given." That is to say, the Incarnation, by its very nature, is an event which affects all time, all places, all men. It cannot be relegated to the past. It has just as important a place in the world's life now, as on that night when the multitude of the heavenly host poured out their "glory to God in the highest."

For, put into the simplest possible form, the Incarnation means God yielding Himself to man; God imparting Himself to man, taking the extreme, the one last step which had not been tried, — appearing as the Word made *flesh*, as the Son of *Man;* and, on this basis of visible contact and companionship, establishing a new relationship of love and saving power. As the sign and beginning of that new communion of life between God and His children, we celebrate that ever-wonderful, ever-beautiful act by which it was inaugurated. In thought, we abide in the fields with the shepherds once more as they keep watch over their flocks by night. In thought, we shrink with them as the angel-figure appears to their spiritual sight, and proclaims the good tidings of great joy. In thought, we suddenly see the sky filled with a shining host, and hear the song that has since sung itself into all the world. In thought, we hear the timid shepherds, as the curtains fall upon their dazed senses, asking each other what these things mean; and climb the ancient terraces with them as they hurry to the little town hard by. And there we search with them, looking for the sign. What sign? "A babe wrapped in swaddling clothes, lying in a manger."

And yet, if our conception of this event be true, — the sign and beginning of a new communion of life between God and the children of men, — the real power and blessing of the Incarnation is greater to-day than it was then.

By its very nature, this new communion gathers in strength and reality the longer it exists. The older it grows, the fresher it becomes. The older it grows, the more it keeps expanding and unfolding itself, both widening and deepening the power of its blessings. So that in a very real and important sense, the Incarnation is more fully and completely a fact to-day than it was when the Babe of Bethlehem was wrapped in swaddling clothes and laid in a manger. The fact, not less than the Child, the fact of God's new relationship with humanity, was in a state of promise, of beginning. But the fact, like the child, was one which was destined to grow.

And see! the ancient prophecy puts the fact of Incarnation as present, — "Unto us a Child is born;" but the power of it, the government which is ultimately to rest on the Child's shoulders, that is not at once; that shall come with growth, with increase.

And very wonderfully, in this single verse, is sketched a succession or progression of states which God comes to assume for humanity and for every individual. Note them: He shall be called: "Wonderful, Counsellor, the Mighty God, the everlasting Father, the Prince of Peace."

As indicating what is to be undertaken in succeeding chapters, let me sketch this progression very briefly as it seems to me to shine out in the Lord's own life in the flesh. We shall then easily see how He successively grows into these different relationships with every man, who is gradually developing under the influence of the incarnate life of God.

At the time of the Lord's birth, what was He to those who looked upon Him? A wonder. He was not yet a Counsellor, a God, a Father, nor a Prince. But He was a wonder. Amazement filled the hearts of these simple shepherds. This child, a Saviour! ay, Christ the Lord! And the Virgin Mother, as she heard them tell of the song in the heavens which had that night been sung, she, too, marvelled, and pondered all these things in her heart. And see! the very narrative tells us how that with the news which the shepherds spread abroad that night, "all they that heard it wondered." To the temple a few days later the Child was carried; and when the aged Simeon uttered his inspired prophecy, "Joseph and His Mother [it is written] marvelled at those things which were spoken of Him." Yes, the Child was indeed a Wonder, the promises and hopes of years centred in Him.

And then what is the next stage or sign of development? In the temple courts He is standing; and now a power of wisdom is shining out of the eager questions and answers which issue from those young lips, filling the gray-beard teachers with astonishment. Once more we see Him standing in the little town of Nazareth, in the old synagogue; and as He finishes His first address, this was the effect it produced: "And all bare Him witness, and wondered at the gracious words which proceeded out of His mouth." Indeed, one of the early questions concerning Him was, "Whence hath this man this wisdom?" The people were astonished at His doctrine. Here, of a truth, was the Counsellor, reading the thoughts of men's hearts, answering the questions which they put to Him, in a manner that often excited their admiration.

But the growth did not stop there. Very lovingly but firmly He began to show forth the power of God, healing the sick, performing many a miracle, and exercising the divine right of forgiving sin. And oftentimes men knelt down to Him in adoration; and sometimes the whole multitude would praise God for all the mighty works which were done by Him. And as the end drew near, the question kept narrowing down more and more as to whether He were not the Son of God; and His enemies accused Him of blasphemy, because they saw more and more clearly that He was filling the functions of the very God of heaven.

But for the disciples, and others who were constantly with Him, He came to fill a place more wonderful and beautiful than that of a God of might. Listen to His conversation on the night of the Last Supper. Note His attitude towards the loving men about Him. There is but one word that will adequately express it, — fatherly. They were reclining about the table, sad at heart because of the treachery and the coming death which He had predicted. Judas rose up and left the room. And when he was gone, the Lord, looking around, we may suppose, upon the men who were there sadly clinging to Him, feeling a fatherly compassion for them, gently said, "Little children, yet a little while I am with you." "Little children!" In His thought and feeling to them, and in theirs to Him, He had become as a Father. They depended upon Him, clung to Him as children would do; and it must have been a moment, which, with all the sorrow, contained also much that was precious, when He could feel it right to say: "Little children."

We might think this was the end; but there is one blessing more, the very fruit, shall we not say, of all, peace, — peace of heart. And nearly the last words which He speaks to His disciples — even after He has called them His children — are, "Peace I leave with you, My peace I give unto you." And His first salutation to them, as they are assembled after the Resurrection, is, "Peace be unto you." And as a sign of the peace which comes by His Spirit, He breathed on them, saying, "Receive ye the Holy Ghost."

Look, then, how beautifully the old prophecy has been fulfilled. Wonderful, Counsellor, Mighty God, Father Everlasting, Prince of Peace! Quietly, step by step, He has ascended into each one of these relationships, until at the close, in that large upper room, He calls those who are about Him His "little children," and gives them His peace.

And yet this is but the sign of the still larger fact which we must ever keep before us. What the Saviour did in the flesh, is the living symbol and pledge of what the incarnate life of God patiently seeks to do for us and for all humanity. I believe this prophecy means, that, step by step, the God-in-Christ will be to the life of humanity what the Saviour, while in the flesh, was to those about Him. And if this be true, then here, in this inspired utterance of the prophet, is a foreshadowing of the history of the growth and development of the truth of the Christ-life in the world of humanity. For as that truth unfolds and gains in acceptance and power, the Child, the Son, the God-with-us, will become, not simply by name, but by experience, the Wonderful, the Counsellor, the Mighty God, the Father Everlasting, the Prince of Peace. Here seems to be divinely expressed a magnificent hope; a sublime expectation; a majestic unfolding of what God's thought and wish towards the world really are.

From the very first, the Lord has been as a Wonder unto many. And yet, it might be shown that even this state has its successive stages. One may be simply in a state of amazed perplexity over the miraculous fact of the Incarnation. One may stand in reverent awe before the thought, the mighty purpose, which the fact discloses. Or one may wonder and praise God for the spiritual power and blessedness, which in some degree he begins to feel as coming from this incarnate life of God. Much of this wonder and reverential awe the Christian Church has felt. Some of it has been mixed with superstitions and errors. But much of it has been simple, earnest, heartfelt wonder. And may we not read in this ancient prophecy, a promise that the world of humanity — meaning by this, not simply the world of religion, but of a thoughtful, patient, truth-loving science, and of a diligent philosophy — shall come to recognize with ever-increasing wonder, God in humanity, as an active, ever-present power in the life of our world.

But we must press on, great as is the temptation to pause and point out some of the signs that this is even now coming to pass. For that is not the end. There are higher levels to which humanity, according to our prophecy, is to rise. I believe this prophecy teaches that a time is coming, when those who seek for spiritual wisdom shall turn with a new power of confidence to Him, of whom it was said, "Never man spake as this Man." I believe that one effect of truer doctrines in the Church will be to send us back all the more directly and trustingly to the life and teaching of Jesus Christ; and that more and more we shall find there "the words of eternal life." Surely we are only in the beginnings of this kind of wisdom. We scarcely realize as yet all that was intended, or the living basis of confidence that was implied, when the Christ said, "Learn of Me." But as we have fuller experience in realizing how this incarnate life does reveal spiritual thoughts, feelings, trials, as no other power of intelligence can, He shall be to us more and more a divine Counsellor; and we shall be able to understand with a new sense of certainty, how, through Him, the Word, the Logos, the very creative Wisdom, was made manifest, and accept from His lips that ever-to-be-remembered testimony: "To this end was I born, and for this cause came I into the world, that I should bear witness to the Truth."

And see! If the Christ-life grows thus in its sublime power of wonder and counsel, the surer are we that He shall exercise yet another power, higher than either, yet growing out of both. The Lord's miracles and beneficent works were often spoken of as signs. Signs of what? The *mighty power of God.* "No man can do these things which Thou doest," men were bound to exclaim, "except God be with Him." And while the Pharisees tried to raise the suspicion that He might be working through evil power, the effort was unavailing. "Can a devil open the eyes of the blind?" it was demanded. And the question was never answered. And when, as seems certain, the Christ-life shall so establish itself among men as to exercise its power to cast out devils, to heal wounds, to restore neglected powers, we shall feel more and more that here is the very might of God.

Dare we hope for anything more? Oh, let us not hesitate to give to this prophecy full scope, and hold it as a promise laid up for humanity, that men, who have learned to feel that in the Lord incarnate there is that manifestation and embodiment of that Divine life, wisdom, power, which cause them to think of Him, as Wonderful, Counsellor, Mighty God, shall also have an inward experience that the communion of life from Him to them, the relation which He sustains to them in every spiritual experience through which they pass, is as near, as tender, as faithful as that which a true father bears to his child.

And then, as the crowning blessing, will come the realization that the Lord is the Prince of Peace; that through His might there are no fears, no temptations, which cannot be subdued; even as the wind and the sea sank into a calm at His command; and that as the last best gift of God to men, there is given to those who have faithfully lived and conquered by His Spirit, a joy and rest of soul which does not pass away but abideth forever.

This same spiritual development might be outlined as applying to our present and individual life and experience. These names, — Wonderful, Counsellor, Mighty God, Father Everlasting, Prince of Peace, — they stand out like great white mile-stones on our spiritual journey. In a life that is growing freely and steadily, they mark clearly defined stages of our spiritual growth.

The Lord, in our first acceptance of Him and in our first efforts to follow Him, should be to us the Wonderful; inspiring simple, delighted, trustful awe for all that He came to do and be. But **He** should come to be our Counsellor; to whom it is still meet we should run and kneel, and ask youth's best question: "What shall I do that I may inherit eternal life." As with his growing life, a young man learns of the men who, by force of arms, or of genius, or of intellect, have been leaders in the world; as ways of knowledge open, and the conflict of human opinion sets him to questioning and even doubting, the greater the need of keeping himself true to one Counsellor, who laid upon youth a simple rule of duty, "If thou wilt enter into life, keep the Commandments."

And then come the labors, not merely nor chiefly of the hands, but of the brain and the heart of manhood; an unsubdued power of selfishness to be grappled with; temptations without number to be resisted; disappointed hopes to be borne; trials to be endured; prosperity, it may be, to be experienced without pride, or selfish indulgence, or the stifling of simple, religious states of trust and love. Ah, how sorely, when we are fairly entered into this battling, baffling period of life, do we need the good right arm of "the Mighty God"!

And when the Lord has been to a man a mighty God in this sense; when evils, which were so hard to meet, gradually are conquered; when, according to the prophetic symbol, the heart of stone, under the wonderful touch of those kindly hands, is changed into a heart of flesh; and the man, for all his hard experiences, becomes more tender, more sensitive to good, more willing to act from that good, then his relations with the Lord must become more as the relation of the disciples with their Master during the last days, when He thought of them, and spoke of them, as "little children." What that inward relationship of love really is, many of us cannot yet know. But a foretaste of it we may have at the communion table; and through that sacramental act, which so beautifully expresses our dependence on Him for whatever is good and true, we may feel and know that there is a communion of life, an interchange, may we not say, of affection and thought; poor and clumsy on our part; strong, tender, undying, on His.

And there, too, in the holy calm that belongs to the communion-hour, — the selfish, worldly thoughts put by, the uncharitable feelings kept down; trying to think, to feel in common what the Lord desires His life to be to us, — there, we may gain some slight experience of what it would be for us to be in such a state of life that the Lord might ever be our Prince of Peace.

Once more recall those names: Wonderful, Counsellor, Mighty God, Father Everlasting, Prince of Peace. And may the Lord be with us in every effort to ascend this shining way!

THE LORD AS THE WONDERFUL

How silently, how silently
   The wondrous gift is given!
So God imparts to human hearts
   The blessings of His heaven.
No ear may hear his coming,
   But in this world of sin,
Where meek souls will receive Him still
   The dear Christ enters in.
PHILLIPS BROOKS.

The Lord as the Wonderful.

✠

"And His name shall be called Wonderful."

✠

WE are to attempt to sketch in this and subsequent chapters the development of the Christ-life in humanity, using as a guide the prophecy which declared that the Child, upon whose shoulder the government shall rest, shall be called Wonderful, Counsellor, the Mighty God, the Father Everlasting, the Prince of Peace. By the "Christ-life" we mean the very Divine Life itself as manifested and brought forth in the person of Jesus Christ our Lord. By "humanity" we mean that life of affection, thought, action, proper to us as human beings. The development of the Christ-life in humanity means, then, in the sense in which we are using these terms, the conscious acceptance in increasing fulness, and on successively higher planes, of the Lord's life in our own.

For consider the very first declaration of this wonderful prophecy: "Unto *us* a Child is born; unto *us* a Son is given." Doubtless, the words were written so, that one generation equally with another might know and believe that the Incarnation, which we may think of as the sign and beginning of a new communion of life between God and His children, was for the sake of all men. And not only that: as expressive of God's near relationship with humanity, the Incarnation exists as an ever-present fact, which makes its appeal to every human being that can be brought to "hear the joyful sound." But by its very nature, this new relationship, this great fact of the "God-with-us," is one which must grow. Gradually, as ways are opened, it must expand and unfold itself. Gradually, as men's hearts grow more friendly towards it, it must widen and deepen the power of its blessings. So that, as has previously been pointed out, while the fact of Incarnation is put as present,— " Unto us a Child *is* born," — the power of it, the government which is to rest on the Child's shoulder, that is not at once, but comes with growth, with increase, mounting up through a succession or progression of states and relationships which God comes to assume for every man, and which are so wonderfully described by these Divine names: Wonderful, Counsellor, Mighty God, Father Everlasting, Prince of Peace.

Here, then, is a fact of immense importance for Christian people to consider: the real and immediate presence of God. Think of the Divine Life as a direct going forth of the creative love and wisdom of God upon every plane and degree of existence. Think of it as raying out from One who so accommodated, and, so to say, extended His infinite nature as to occupy, and thus include within Himself, this plane of existence in which we now are; rather than as proceeding from One so remote from our present conditions that He cannot be touched with a feeling of our infirmities, cannot, from any experience within Himself, know our frame and remember that we are dust. For that nearer and more immediate communion of life is what was accomplished ultimately by the Incarnation. The birth of Jesus Christ, the ministry of Jesus Christ, was not the coming of a Person separate from God, who should take His place, nor act even as a kind of champion for us. Think of this, rather, as the one long promised, long expected means by which the Divine should become God-with-us.

See! This Humanity, for all it was so like our humanities in the experiences which it voluntarily shared with the children of men, was, as we believe, and as the Gospels declare, conceived, not of man, but of the Holy Spirit. In conception, that which is slowly developed into a human being, or soul, is a living organism, composed of altogether spiritual substances. Gradually that primitive form, or spiritual mind, becomes enveloped and protected within successive clothings, until the mother, from the substances of the natural world, silently weaves the swathes and coverings which are to serve as a natural or physical body, and make possible its entrance into this outer world. But when we speak of the Incarnation, we are carefully to remember that this primitive form was not, as with us, derived from a human father, but was formed or moulded by the Divine; formed, as with men, of those altogether invisible and purest substances of the spiritual world; formed, therefore, we may be sure, with a perfection never present with us, and with a richness and fulness of spiritual good and truth, which also marks a distinction between that and all other humanities in their first state at birth. Moreover, we are ever to remember that the very inmost, that which in us first receives life from the Divine, and is above the plane of our consciousness, was in the Lord's Humanity not a created form recipient of life, as with man, but it was the very Divine Life itself.

In first principles, then, the Humanity, we may say, was Divine. Without the usual agency of a human fatherhood, and thus, avoiding the taint and limitations which go with such a fatherhood, and which are never wholly obliterated, these primitive and altogether invisible substances; these first things in the creation of a human organism, were divinely gathered and moulded into that primitive form which the Virgin Mary clothed with a body. More richly stored than with any man; pure and true with the purity and truth belonging to the heavens; gathered and formed by a power of wisdom that does not err, this initial or primitive mind was indeed, as the Gospels declare, a "holy thing." Only in the outer clothing of the natural mind and in the successive wrappings furnished by the woman-nature, did it share our weakness. But primarily, essentially, it was born with the capacity of becoming Divine, through the removal of whatever was imperfect or limiting and through complete union with the Divine.

And now think of this mind and nature to which we give the general name "Humanity," formed, we may properly say, under the Divine auspices, not avoiding the way of entrance into this world by which we all have come, and yet taking its start, receiving its very first or primitive form, from the very Divine Itself,— think of this Humanity as specially created that it might become the perfect instrument by which the Divine might come and dwell among us. Through many ages Jehovah God had filled angels with His Spirit, and so had made Himself present throughout the universal heavens. And mediately through the heavens, His Spirit had gone forth to the sons of men. But a time came, according to prophecy, when a cloud of iniquity spread itself between God and humanity, so dark, so dense, as to become almost impenetrable to the purer influences from above. And then the Lord God took the last, the extreme step; "bowed the heavens," as the Scripture expresses it, "and came down," — not as at Sinai, with lightning-flash and thunder-clap; not by suddenly standing upon the earth in the fulness of His glory; but, as the Scriptures had long ago declared, by the seed of a woman, — by the formation and birth of the Humanity of Jesus Christ, to be the special instrument, by which in time the very love and wisdom and spirit of God might gradually come down into these humbler planes of life in which men dwell, and become so established in them as henceforth always to exert an immediate and saving influence upon them.

Very like our humanities, in all that pertains to the growth of the natural body and the natural mind, was the Humanity of our Lord. The same tenderness and helplessness of the infantile body; the same possibility of weariness, hunger, thirst, pain; the same exposure, too, in the lower planes of the mind, to the assaults of evil, resulting in internal struggle, temptation, and combat. And yet, while humbly, ay, most gratefully acknowledging this strange likeness, which makes such appeal to our faith and love, we should never forget that *un*likeness, that difference, by which the Lord could be not simply Son of Man, ("man of sorrows and acquainted with grief!"), but also, in the strictest and highest sense, Son of God, having all power in heaven and on earth. We should ever remember that, differently from us, that primitive form or mind, around which the mother simply weaves the clothings proper to the natural world, was divinely begotten. In it, therefore, was no such limitation or inherent imperfection as belongs to us. Rather, it was born with the capacity of becoming divine, through union with the Divine, and through the removal of what, in a relative sense, we speak of as imperfections. For even "the heavens are not clean in His sight."

And so we think of this Humanity of Jesus Christ as so formed and born as to be able to serve as a perfect instrument by which the Lord God might come and dwell among us; might so express and adapt His love; might so shape and accommodate His truth; might, in a word, so set Himself to our human conditions and needs, as to establish Himself in this plane of existence, and forever after sustain a relationship as near and immediate to men of the earth as to angels of highest heaven.

Gradually this was accomplished. Gradually the Divine Life of love and wisdom came into the several planes which by incarnation existed in the Humanity of Jesus Christ, removed whatever was limiting or imperfect in them, and made them Divine. First, those which were inmost or highest, and on a line, may we not say, with the life of the holiest angels; then those next below. And thus in this invisible and quiet way, the Divine kept coming down into these planes of life in which angels are; established Himself in those degrees, making them Divine in Himself, removing every least imperfection, filling them, glorifying them, making them one with Himself.

And later on, this same process began to take place in the lower degrees of thought and affection, — those in which we now are. And here the process was more slow. For here, there were more imperfections. Here, too, there was a stronger appearance of separateness from the God from whom the Humanity was living. Here were direct assaults from evil spirits; here were experienced the despising and rejecting of men; here, amid depths of sorrow and anguish which we cannot fathom, was the putting away of every least thought or wish which loving friends, which cruel enemies, which bodily dangers, ay, which " the pains of hell " could prompt, and which looked to self-vindication, to self-preservation even. And here, in these lower planes of thought and affection, which we find it so difficult to even moderately control, and which lie so near to the senses of the body, as easily to be seduced by its fallacies and appetites, — here, too, was carried on that same process, which we have thought of as taking place in the higher or heavenly degrees. Every imperfection, every human or earthly limitation was removed, until here, too, in the planes of life in which we now are, not excepting even the physical, the divine of the Lord became established. These degrees of life were made divine in Himself; so that His last words to the world were: "Lo, I am with you always." And this, too, is His promise: "Where two or three are gathered together in my name, there am I in the midst of them." "In the midst," — not spiritually far away, but right here in these very planes and degrees in which we are thinking and feeling.

Whether the explanations which have been offered in this chapter have in any way helped to make this great and fundamental doctrine of the Incarnation of the Humanity of Jesus Christ more intelligible to the reader, we cannot know. But if anything has been said which has made this truth seem a little clearer, I am sure we shall agree as to why, in that brief but expressive list of names, the significance of which we are to study, the very first appellation to be applied to the Child of Bethlehem, should be "the Wonderful." Wonderfully, indeed, was He given; and wonderful the purpose for which He came. Even those who knew no more than that a Saviour had been born felt something of that strange wonder with which even now we turn to this ever-living fact. Amazement filled the hearts of the simple shepherds. And all to whom they broke the news that night wondered. Joseph marvelled, as the aged Simeon, with the child in his arms, poured out the prophecy concerning Him. But with an awe yet deeper, the Virgin mother, from whose lips I doubt not we have all these tender narratives of the birth and early days; she, "the highly favored," kept all these things and pondered them in her heart.

And the thought comes: We must not let the wonderfulness die out of this ever-blessed story. In the present unwillingness to accept as truth anything which cannot be demonstrated to be such to or by the senses; in the present craze for evolving truth out of the collected experiences of mankind, and ignoring, as childish, truths and knowledges which are given as a revelation from above, we shall do well to remember that it was declared of the Child of Bethlehem, "His name shall be called, Wonderful." We would not keep the Incarnation as a mystery. We believe that it is possible for the spiritual intelligence to see the truthfulness of it. We believe it is even possible for the spiritual intelligence to understand in a degree how the Incarnation could be true. But even for such, the fact, the Child, the near and perfect relationship into which the Lord has come, should awaken and keep awake a sense of wonder. These words are written, well knowing that the natural reason of man, which looks no further than to nature for causes, is by instinct sceptical of anything which presents itself as a distinctly spiritual fact; and that those who look no further than into the substances of nature for the origins of life, are declaring the impossibility of the virgin-birth. But remember, we are standing merely on the plane of *effects*, not causes; and he is but a sensualist who will not let his thought, his faith, rise to a plane of life and of truth where the senses, instead of asserting themselves as masters, are well content to be as servants, bringing to the spiritual intelligence such materials as are available for the illustration and confirmation of divine things.

To preserve a faith in the actuality of the Divine, to stand before it in reverence, is surely a blessing, and one which, under right conditions, cannot but exert a powerful influence upon the inner workings of a man's life. To lose that faith, — for one may lose it, — to turn to nature or to self as a god, is to shut up the heaven of the soul. Revere the highest! Revere the best! Have faith in the wonderful!

And somehow this hope comes: although many may not acknowledge with their lips the Divinity of the Lord; although they may not in their thought rationally perceive it, still, to nearly every man or woman who at heart is trying to lead the Christian life, the Saviour is inwardly cherished as the Wonderful; the fullest, the most perfect embodiment of the divine life among men. Call Him a man among men; and yet there is no Christian but would deem it a sacrilege to claim equality with Jesus of Nazareth. Something here that is different; that never seems to lose its perfect height; something that men keep coming back to with new questions, with fresh explanations; something that affords a view of the Divine Life as it can be seen nowhere else; something that keeps drawing out the deepest confidences of the human heart. It is well so; for, as the Psalmist says, "The fear [that is, the reverence] of the Lord is the beginning of wisdom." First, "the Wonderful." Let the children's first thought and knowledge of Him who came even as a child, be of His perfect wisdom and love. Let them feel that through Baptism they are to bear His Name, and as the old baptismal service puts it, "continue Christ's faithful soldiers and servants unto their life's end." Other names will be spoken into their ears, as youth advances; the deeds of many a hero whom the world holds dear in its memory will be recounted. Shall these dim the brightness of that earlier vision of perfect life? The gentleness, the truth, the faithfulness of it; the holiness of purpose; the revelation made here of what God is and of what man should be; of the power of self-sacrifice, of the sacredness of service,—shall He who embodied all this and more than this, ever cease to be to our thought "the Wonderful?" And if we should see in Him something more than man, than hero, than example; if we should see in His Humanity the perfect instrument, "conceived of the Holy Ghost, born of the Virgin Mary," capable of being glorified and of being the means by which the very Divine Life of love and wisdom could gain and forever retain an immediate presence with men on earth,—would the wonder grow any less? For such, has not the Psalmist rightly spoken: "I will remember the works of the Lord: surely I will remember thy wonders of old?"

THE LORD AS THE COUNSELLOR.

In the way that He shall choose
   He will teach us,
Not a lesson we shall lose,
   All shall reach us.

Strange and difficult indeed
   We may find it,
But the blessing that we need
   Is behind it.

All the lessons He shall send
   Are the sweetest,
And His training, in the end,
   Is completest.
HAVERGAL.

The Lord as the Counsellor.

✠

"And His name shall be called . . . Counsellor."

✠

BY the Lord as the Counsellor, we think of Him with special reference to His making the Divine Truth known to men. With the ordinary teacher, we should think of this as involving the learning of facts and principles, rationally apprehending them, and then imparting them to others. We should think of the teacher as one who serves as a mediator between Truth on the one hand, and those who are in ignorance of it on the other. Moreover we should think of the Truth as not only separate from, but as superior to the Teacher.

Now, turn for a moment to the Gospel of St. John. As the apostles linger about the table of the Last Supper, weighed down by the thought that He is to be betrayed and withdrawn from them, He, trying to revive their drooping spirits, tells them that although He is going from their sight, He is in reality going to prepare a place for them, where, by a way which they know, they may rejoin Him. And one honest soul, not ashamed to show his ignorance, and feeling, no doubt, that he would rather keep Him as He was with them there than run this chance of a reunion after death, bluntly declares that they know neither the place nor the way of which He is speaking. We can easily imagine that this declaration was either openly or silently acquiesced in by all. And here did indeed seem to be a fatal obstacle to that quiet certainty of heart, which the Lord was trying to establish among them. Here was that spirit of doubt and spiritual ignorance, which so often springs up in the human heart, and just as the Divine consolations seem likely to become complete, and the portal of death is quietly swinging open to reveal itself as a way to eternal life, waives faith back, and cries, as if to one who has disappeared behind that portal, "We know not whither thou goest; and how can we know the way?"

What feelings that cry of Thomas awakened in the Lord's heart, as they sat there on that last night, in the quiet upper chamber, who shall tell? Three years He had taught Thomas Didymus and his fellow-disciples. What more could be said? "We know not whither Thou goest; and how can we know the way?" There they seemed to have to part from Him. And then, as they listened, there was made an answer far more wonderful than the promise He had just held out to them. Few and simple the words are; and yet no saint, no sage, no reformer, no prophet, nor seer of whom we have ever heard, has thought to utter those words. Ponder them! "I am the Way, the Truth, and the Life."

It has been the claim of many a wise and devout man, that he could point out the right way; could make known the truth; could lead the inquirer to the true source of life. But who has ever deliberately said: "I am the Way, the Truth, the Life?" We will narrow our inquiry down to the one term which immediately concerns our subject. Who has ever said, "*I am the Truth!*" Truth, which in its purest and naked principles exists neither with men, nor angels, but with God only! Truth, which is the order itself underlying the Lord's Kingdom; nay, which is the veriest reality in the universe; the form of the very Divine Love or Life, forever guiding it in its creative, regenerating work; that internal light, yea, that substance of substances, by the reception of which man becomes man! Think of Truth in this its large and exalted meaning, and not simply as a little book-knowledge, or some pet idea or doctrine which one has fondly labelled as "truth," and then turn to this Figure who quietly says, "I am the Truth!"

Do we say or think, "The Lord could not have used this language in so important a sense." Ah, was it not the case that men's thoughts and interpretations were always falling far short of His meaning? And do we imagine that in this instance we are a little ahead of Him; and that He little knew what was involved in this identity between Himself and the Truth? And was He also falling short of the full meaning of His words when He said: "I am the Light of the world!" or, "The words that I speak unto you, they are spirit and they are life?" Was He speaking below the range of our best thought, when He made His identity with the Truth the very ground of His divine royalty, saying to the Roman governor, "To this end was I born, and for this cause came I into the world, that I should bear witness to the Truth"?

Here, now, is a subject of immense importance: the Lord's relation to the Truth. By the promise of Scripture; by the experiences of the Christian Church, whose very existence rests upon that Kingdom of the Truth of which He declared Himself to be King; by the testimony of the hearts of many generations who have turned to Him for the words of eternal life, the Lord has been pre-eminently man's spiritual Counsellor. Eighteen centuries have but verified this claim. In all that appertains to spiritual life, there is no Christian man but must feel that in some degree the Lord is his Teacher. We say "in some degree," because all may not see alike the extent, nor the real basis of this claim. The Lord stands before Christian men to-day as the One of all others who can show them the way of spiritual life, who can teach them the

Truth. Why? By what right? What gave Him the right to say; "Heaven and earth shall pass away, *but my words shall not pass away?*" And yet the history of human thought upon every subject of knowledge is a constant shifting from one form and statement and belief to another, — new facts brought to the eye; old ones seen in new relations and in new light. And yet that claim put forth in the realization of such changes, — "heaven and earth *shall* pass away," — confidently asserting the immutability of the judgments of His mouth, — "my words shall *not* pass away!" Again we ask, upon what does such a claim rest? How can we know that the truths which the Lord taught are the very truths which He thought them to be? How, to point our question still more directly to the special subject before us, can we know that the Lord is, of all others who ever have been or ever may be, the supreme, the absolutely sure teacher in spiritual and divine things, so as to be not only in name but in very fact our Counsellor?

Do not imagine for a moment that such questions are asked from any love of discussion. Nor let us say, This is not a "practical" subject; it does not affect me in my present spiritual condition with its vexations, cares, conflicts. If we would make and keep our religion practical it must be founded on reality, — not book-knowledge simply; not sentiment merely; but fact, truth. The Christ declares himself to be that reality, that fact, that Truth. Ascertain that; see it to be so; and our religion shall not float in air, shall not moulder away in books, shall not dream itself away in weakly sentiment. It shall be founded upon a Rock. So that when the rains descend, and the floods come, and the winds blow and beat upon our spiritual house. it shall not fall because founded upon a Rock.

Strive we then to understand, not so much how the Lord knew Truth, as how, and in what sense, He became Truth, so that he could declare His identity with it. And here I must ask the reader to recall what was presented in the preceding chapter, as to the assumption and the nature of the Humanity born into the world. The very primitive form, or, as we have spoken of it, "initiament," around which the substances of the natural world were woven by the mother in the form of a physical body; that was not material, was not natural, did not even have the limitations which inevitably adhere to one derived of a human fatherhood. With every individual, that first form or beginning of the human organism is distinctly spiritual, and is composed of spiritual substances. Around this are successively formed the swathes and coverings of the natural mind and spiritual body, and, outermost of all, the natural or physical body.

But in the conception and birth of the Humanity of our Lord, that first or primitive form was not derived from a human father, but was formed or moulded by the Divine; formed, as with men, of those altogether invisible and purest substances of the spiritual or heavenly world; formed, therefore, we may be sure, with a perfection never present with us, and with a richness and fulness of spiritual good and truth, which also marks a distinction between that and all other human natures in their first state at birth. This Humanity was thus formed and born in order that it might be the perfect instrument by which the very Divine Love and Wisdom could become known, established, and thus be immediately present on every plane and degree of angelic and of human life. To put it in another way, it was the one instrument by which God could think and feel in just the plane of life in which we are thinking and feeling, or in which angels think and feel; and, as a result of bringing His Divine Love and Wisdom into these human and angelic planes, and establishing them there, becoming immediately present in them.

And now, do we not begin to see what we are searching for: how the Humanity of the Lord could become Divine Truth, so that He could say, "I am the Truth"? Simply, — for in this view of it, it is simple, — by the Divine Wisdom coming down successively into each one of the degrees of that nature, from highest to lowest, removing every slightest imperfection in them, and establishing itself in those planes or degrees of life.

We have had occasion to notice that as a process, this descent of the Divine into the degrees of the Human first took place in those which were highest. Let me illustrate. We will think of that plane of angelic life, the highest, in which they dwell of whom it is said, "They always behold the face of my Father who is in heaven." Such are represented by the Lord as being in spiritual association with little children; drawn to them no doubt because of their love for what is pure and innocent. Love, mercy, peace, innocence, — these are all qualities of that celestial plane of being. By creation every mind has that degree of life; and if he will but carry the work of regeneration far enough so as really to become in spirit a little child, he will come into the full use and enjoyment of that degree after death. But the quality of that life, pure as it is, is not Divine. It is angelic, celestial; but not Divine. It has its limitations. And by making that plane of life Divine in the Humanity of the Lord, we mean the removal of those limitations, so that on that plane love was perfect, absolute, — God's own love.

See! the parable of the Prodigal Son will

help us. We might think of the relative difference between the perfect love of our Heavenly Father and the highest form of celestial love, as being something like the difference between the father's and the elder brother's love for the profligate who had come home in shame. Such unconditional forgiveness; such absolute love; such joy over the boy who has come back in tatters, without a word of bitterness, or of wounded love, — that was something which the elder brother, for all his fidelity and virtue, could not understand. And something like this same difference exists, doubtless, between the love of the highest angels and the Saviour-love of God, who is kind to the unthankful and to the evil, and sendeth rain on the just and on the unjust. Think you they could enter into the depths of that love which took this strange way of coming to men; which could love on through every form of shame or abuse; which felt no bitterness; desired no vindication; encircled, yet forced itself upon no one; lent itself, spent itself freely, utterly, for the good of all men! Why, this love of saving, of building up, of giving joy, of reciprocal union,—this is the very Divine Life itself. God, and God alone, is such Life.

And just as on this highest or celestial plane of life, so on every succeeding plane or degree, the limitations and imperfections peculiar to each were, in the Lord's Humanity, put off, and the perfect love and wisdom of the Divine, keyed, we might say, so as to be in harmony with it, were substituted and established. And this same process included even the degrees of life in which the natural mind of man is. And here of course the imperfections were much greater, and the substitution of Divine for human ways of thinking and feeling much more difficult and slow. And yet as the way was prepared, the

Divine of the Lord came down into these planes no less than the higher ones, and made them Divine. We think and feel as men; the Lord, standing in our place, and amid our conditions, learned to think and feel, and does so now, *as God.*

And so, in this marvellous yet ever silent, hidden way, step by step, in every degree of human life, the Lord, first thinking and feeling as the angels and as we do, gradually put away all the limiting things of their and of our thought and affection, and then came to think and to feel divinely. And with this glimpse of the change which was wrought in His Humanity, what a new power of meaning there is in such language as "The words that I speak unto you, I speak *not of myself;*" "My doctrine is *not mine*, but His that sent me;" "I can of *Mine own self* do nothing!" The apparent duality all disappears. The Lord is telling us that the wisdom and the power are not such as can be spoken of as belonging to a human state. They are not, as men are fond of saying, the result of any "natural development." Rather they are the very Divine Wisdom and power of Love accommodated to and brought down into these human planes of thought and affection. "If I bear witness of Myself, My witness is not true." Here, may we not say, is His way of telling us that by no amount of natural development or self-intelligence could Divine Truth be set forth before men. On the other hand, His witness is true, because the wisdom from which He speaks is the Divine Wisdom come down in Him into the planes of our human life.

To one to whom this doctrine of the Divine Humanity appears as true, how perfectly it explains the Lord's meaning when He said, "I am the Truth." Nay, more, how it establishes the ground of Christian confidence! The Lord's words are true, because He speaks not of Himself, — not from any intelligence resulting, as men are apt to think, from long intellectual training or a power of self-derived intelligence, but from a wisdom which is Divine.

And yet, to know how this was is only for the sake of knowing that it is. Little the people knew, as they thronged about Him to hear Him tell of the Kingdom of Heaven, how it was that He had such wisdom. And yet they came to Him with their questions; marvelled at His teachings; and rightly said, "Never man spake like this man." And if, though dimly as yet, we may understand some of the things which then were hidden, it surely must be to the end that more confidently, more unreservedly even than the people of old, we may go to Him for the words of eternal life.

To know that the Lord, by that work of glorification which was carried on in His Humanity, became the Divine Truth; that what

He has told us about our present lives, our spiritual needs, about eternal life, about the Divine Providence must be true because it was Truth Speaking! Amid the changing of opinions; the man-made religions which spring up, and totter, and fall; amid the false Christs and false prophets which beckon for a following, how precious, how restful this blessed certainty which still quietly stands among us! We who may be asking, "What shall I do that I may inherit eternal life?" we who may be saying with Philip, "Show us the Father;" we who in some failure, or sin, or travail of soul may some day feel the need of the Divine consolations, and the word and the touch of One whom we feel to be true, forget not where Truth is.

> "Amid the weak, One strong,
> Amid the false One true,
> Amid all change, One changing not, —
> One hope we ne'er shall rue.

. . . .

In whose sight all is Now,
In whose love all is best:
The things of this world pass away, —
Come, let us in Him rest."

THE LORD AS THE MIGHTY GOD.

"THE very God! think, Ahib; dost thou think?
So the All-Great, were the All-Loving too —
So, through the thunder comes a human voice
Saying, 'O heart I made, a heart beats here!
Face My hands fashioned, see it in Myself.
Thou hast no power nor may'st conceive of mine,
But love I gave thee, with Myself to love,
And thou must love Me who have died for thee!'"

BROWNING.

The Lord as the Mighty God.

✢

"And His name shall be called . . . the mighty God."

✢

TO be able to read these few words and feel that they are made true through the life and nature of our Lord Jesus Christ, is a triumph, surely, of Christian faith. "Believe in God; believe also in Me," our Lord exclaimed. The God-like and the Christian-like, — were they not linked together? "My Lord *and* my God!" Into the mind of the awestruck Thomas, God and the living Lord entered through one single thought. "Beware," wrote the Tarsus Jew, "lest any man spoil you through philosophy and vain deceit, after the tradition of men, after the rudiments of the world, and not after Christ. For in Him dwelleth all the fulness of the Godhead bodily." From their worship of "the unknown God," the Athenians were exhorted to turn the thoughts of their hearts to Him by whom God was become God-manifest.

And so it has been throughout the history of the Christian Church; so it is now. Some portion, at least, of His followers, associating their thoughts of Him with their thoughts of God, and when they looked for Divine help in meeting their trials or resisting their evils, turning instinctively to Him who invited just this kind of approach and appeal when He said, "Come unto Me all ye that labor and are heavy laden." Men's thoughts of this Saviour-Lord have not been always clear,— are not now. They have often been widely different. And yet it would seem as if there have always been some who have found common ground in simply thinking of the Lord as the Saviour of their souls; as One who stands related to them and to their inmost thoughts and feelings and needs, as would be impossible to any man or angel. To Him in trial-hours their thoughts have turned. His name has rested on their lips as they "fell asleep." By Him they have been cheered and strengthened. From Him has come a peace which passeth all understanding; as if once again He trod upon life's sea, and to the winds and the waves cried, "Peace, be still!"

Very wonderful, very beautiful, and, we have no right to doubt, very real has been and still is this simple looking, this heart-clinging to the Friend of publicans and sinners. What pains have been and are endured in this name! What struggles against the sins of one's heart have been and still are carried on because of Him! The history of Christ the Lord, as He has lived it again and again in men's hearts, who shall write us that? The thoughts He has illumined; the longings

He has inspired; the maimed, the blind, the palsied things of our nature on which He has laid those kindly hands; the dead thoughts and feelings that have come to life through Him; the possession and tormentings of devils that have been brought to an end! Again we say, who shall write for us this spiritual history of the Saviour Lord, with its lowly beginnings; its gentle counsellings; man's doubting and adoring; the following and forsaking; the selfish and evil things in us trying to silence, to arrest, to kill and bury Him out of sight; and then, for some, after severe temptation, the coming forth in still greater power and deathless victory!

Very real this spiritual history is, too real to be overlooked or denied in any attempt to understand the Redeemer's life. Indeed, it seems certain that it is this spiritual help and reality of the Son of Man which has kept and still keeps Him in an altogether different position and relation with us from any other being of whom men have knowledge. How has faith in the Redeemer so persistently endured, when urged under the form of dogmas which appear to be so foreign to the real truth of the Gospel? Think of the intolerance, the persecutions, the abuse of spiritual power through the lust of dominion, which have brought such misery into the Church itself, and engendered such *un*Christ-like thoughts and feelings. See the Church of to-day divided, bearing different names; more tolerant, perhaps, and yet each sect jealous of its respective doctrines, practices, and titles; all claiming, it may be, a desire for unity, but certainly not formed into that united and altogether loving communion into which surely the Church of Christ shall some day come.

And then, how strange it seems that the power of the Redeemer's life should have endured through all these things; strange, until its spiritual reality is remembered; until it is recognized as exerting an influence upon the spiritual life of man, having still the power to call out trust, to comfort, to inspire, to remove evil. That this power is what it might be and yet will be, if with truer thoughts and humbler hearts we would turn to its living source, is not for a moment pretended. But even then, this remains: if the spiritual experiences of pure and devoted followers, some of them known to us, but many more, whose names, uncelebrated, are yet written in heaven, — if these inward experiences are true, this fact is certain: there has been from the beginning and still is an influence, a power of the Spirit, which radiates from the risen and glorified Lord, and which, through the experiences of those whose hearts have been opened to it, attest not simply its reality, but its uplifting, life-giving power. While the scholar is "weighing the evidences" as to the authenticity of this or that passage; while the theologian is at work on the "formulas of faith," yonder man, who is trying to meet some trial, or to be faithful in some duty, or seeking protection from some evil, turning humbly, trustfully, appealingly to his Saviour, and into whose heart there comes a new feeling of courage, of pure desire, of protection, — that man, is he not gaining a living testimony of the loving presence and power of the Redeemer's life? Something of this there has always been, from the moment that the Saviour, in being withdrawn from outward gaze, said, "Lo, I am with you always." And this it is, which, supported by the simple story of the Gospels, has, in spite of false teachings, abuses, denials, kept the Godliness of Christ as a fact among those who take His name. It is a part of the history of the Christ-life which cannot be forgotten nor lightly put aside. Though we ourselves should have had but little of this inward experience, that does not render us free to ignore or to make light of the testimony of those who have.

And more: It is, we are convinced, from this side, rather than from doctrinal argument, that the sole Divinity of the Lord Jesus Christ can best be approached. For of this we may well be sure: the presentation of a doctrine, however true, is but one step in the formation of faith. For faith is an inward thing. Essentially it is a state of interior confidence, resulting from a preception that a thing is true. Not always does such a faith express itself in words, nor even in a well-ordered series of thoughts. To have faith as a grain of mustard-seed is not, necessarily, to have a belief concerning God which is theologically exact; but it is, in simple, heartfelt confidence, to do the things which the Lord declares to be right, humbly, faithfully, religiously. If a man has that kind of faith and really practises it, what mountains of selfish love may he not have removed! True doctrine helps to make plain to a man's thought the confidence he feels. To that extent it enlarges and strengthens it. It gives it form. It enables him to examine and understand it. The man feels fortified. False doctrine, on the other hand, may confuse, and may even make faith blind. But in either case it is essential to remember that faith is dependent upon an internal disposition and inclination, and not simply upon theological or doctrinal statements. No wonder, then, that we should find the Lord saying: "No man can come unto Me except the Father which hath sent Me draw him;" words which, in their simplest meaning, may well teach us that man cannot be driven to accept the Lord as a Saviour by any outside power of argument, nor by doctrine alone, nor by human exhortation alone.

And so, while the subject of the Lord as the mighty God might, of all others which we shall consider, seem to suggest a theological treatment, it has appeared to us that the most hopeful side from which to approach it is this side of spiritual experience upon which we have chiefly dwelt. The favorite texts on which we rely for proof of the Lord's Divinity might easily be brought together. Nor would it be difficult to show how, if we deny this Divinity, we actually compromise the Son of Man, — make Him declare things concerning His divine descent and union with the Father; make Him claim powers and assume relations with mankind, which were either a dream, an exaggeration, or a deception. But the texts and the arguments are familiar. We should not gain much by another use of them. Besides, in the two preceding chapters, we have tried to state with some degree of particularity some things which might be of help, not in proving this Divinity, but in enabling us to see, if possible, how the Lord could and did assume a human nature; how it was a perfect instrument by which the Divine Love and Wisdom would come down and become established in all the successive planes of angelic and human life; and how, because of such a coming, God is immediately and savingly near to all men. This much, as an aid to clearer thinking, have we tried to do. But far more desirous should we be to learn some of the spiritual results of this presence; to know something about this influence, this power, that we associate with the Lord. And if we can see that it has a power over evil,— that now, as in the days of old, it is the one force that can set us really free from the devils of our nature; can cure, can .bless, can forgive,—shall we not be learning in the best of ways that the Lord was indeed rightly called in prophecy "the Mighty God"?

And here is a point worth remembering: the people's thoughts of the Lord as divine, and the Lord's power over evil, are invariably associated together. Nay, there is something more remarkable yet: evil spirits themselves recognized His power as divine! "What have we to do with Thee, Jesus of Nazareth? . . . I know Thee who Thou art; the *Holy One of God.*" What was it provoked the Pharisees, so that they accused Him of blasphemy? He was sitting in a house teaching, when through an opening in the roof a helpless cripple on his pallet was let down at His feet. And looking at that sufferer as he lay there before Him, He quietly said: "Man, thy sins be forgiven Thee." And instantly the thought arose in the minds of many of the bystanders, "Who is this which speaketh blasphemies? *Who can forgive sins but God alone?*" He was sitting in a Pharisee's house. The customary bathing of the feet, the kiss of salutation, the anointing, — all had been omitted; until the sinful woman knelt down at those feet and wept, and kissed and poured oil upon them. And He who came to call sinners to repentance said to the woman: "Thy sins are forgiven." But the Pharisees, and those who sat at meat, said, "Who is this that forgiveth sins also?"

Oh, how often was that word "forgive" on those lips! How often was He giving release from some bondage of evil! How closed and hardened and embittered the life of the little publican of Jericho had been, until one day the Friend of publicans stood at his door; and to the amazement, we doubt not, of the despised man whose soul opened to this new influence of love that had sought it, declared, what God alone has the right to declare: "This day is salvation come to this house."

Let us seriously consider this feature of the Saviour's ministry. When He stated His Divine character and descent, many were mystified, many were offended; and there were always some ready with an argument with which to try and humble Him. When they saw some of His miracles, they were amazed; and some were ready to declare that one of the prophets was come back to them. But when they heard Him forgive men of their sins, when evil spirits were made subject to His word, then the thought of God came instantly into their minds. "It was never so seen in Israel," the multitude exclaimed in awe, as the dumb man was delivered of his evil tormentor. In vain some of the rulers pretended that He was working from evil power. Would a kingdom so divided against itself stand? But this let them remember: "If I cast out devils by the spirit of God, then the kingdom of God is come unto you." "By the Spirit of God!" To Him, then, to the people, to the spirits of darkness, this power over evil was the surest sign of the presence of a Divine Power. And that fact we may safely enlarge so as to include our own spiritual experiences. When, through the Lord's power, any evil is removed, repented of, put away, forgiven, then may we justly feel that for us, at least, the prophecy has been fulfilled: "His Name shall be called the Mighty God."

The power that conquers evil is the Lord's power. First, by showing us what evil is. This we must have noticed: while the Lord was ever ready to forgive, while He tried to lead those who were in sin to feel that with Divine help they could live in newness of life, He never condoned evil. He never said of it, as some try to say of it, "It is only an appearance." He never called it, as some are trying to call it, "undeveloped good." Is not this more nearly His estimate? Evil is life perverted; it is using for self-gratification the powers and blessings which were intended for unselfish joy and usefulness. That kind of life is the very opposite of the Divine Life. That kind of life, persisted in, results in ever-increasing selfishness, in inordinate indulgence, in a complete turning away from God. Such associate themselves with those who are in similar delights of evil, — not only with men, but still more intimately with evil spirits, whose delight it is to encourage these selfish loves, and fill them with burnings and jealousies. "He that committeth sin is the servant of sin." Evil is enslaving, debasing, weakening. Life thus perverted brings unhappiness, suffering. Very significant is the fact that the Lord so often associated sin with disease. Why say to the sick of the palsy, "Thy sins be forgiven," but that in the Lord's sight the helpless body of the man before Him was a perfect image of a helpless condition of the spirit into which sin may finally bring man. And why, when they were complaining about His eating with publicans and sinners, should He say, "They that are whole need not a physician, but they that are sick"? Was it not, in part, at least, that we might know that evil does injure the soul; and that, if unremoved, the mind becomes vitiated and unfitted for the kind of life for which it was intended?

And then the Lord's treatment of those in sin. He was ever ready to forgive: but did He ever spare them, if we must use that word, the knowledge of their sinfulness? Did He ever say to any such, "You are the victim of circumstances; this evil of yours is not as bad as it seems"? Was not the first step always a confession of sin, seeing it in its true light, and then abjuring it? And then was not the next step a looking to the Lord, and an effort to walk in the new way which He had opened before them? Were they not led to feel that the power by which they were delivered was a holy power? "If I *by the Spirit of God* cast out devils!" Was not that the experience? Nothing out of the sinner's own life. No "native good," as some fondly say, suddenly flattered into life and growing so prodigiously, as by its sheer bulk to crowd out evil.

The woman weeping at His feet; the man of Gadara sitting quietly by his Redeemer; Zaccheus; Peter, as he sinks upon his knees with the cry, "Depart from me, for I am a sinful man, O Lord," — all these seem to bear one common testimony. They have been in evil; they are bitterly aware of their sinfulness; but through the Lord a change has come, a deliverance has been wrought, a new life begun.

And to-day, is there any true deliverance

to be gained from evil except by seeing its sinfulness; turning from it, and with the Lord's help trying to live in newness of life? Know we of any power greater than that by which the Lord our Redeemer triumphed, and helped others to triumph? There is much hiding of evil; covering it up with little social graces and proprieties; holding it in bounds through motives of prudence and expediency. But who does not know that that is not deliverance from evil? Who does not know that that brings no true rest? The Lord's way is the one sure way. To any and all who are conscious of some evil, might we not feel that the Lord says this: "Do not try to excuse the evil. Do not try to make it appear less than it is. Do not try to lay the blame of it at somebody's door. Confess the wickedness of it. Confess that it is a transgression of the divine laws of life which I have taught you. But do not fear:

if you desire to be free, turn to Me; I will strengthen your heart. And when the evil returns, firmly say, 'I do not will this, because it is a sin against the Lord.' So, little by little, you shall receive a new power to do good; will feel an ever-increasing joy in it; and will be led into the way of peace."

. . . . . .

See how beautifully the Lord's life is intended to develop among us: First, He calls out our wonder, our admiration, our reverence: " His Name shall be called Wonderful." Then when we begin to wish to know more about life and its duties, He presents Himself as our Guide, our Teacher, the Divine Truth Itself: " His name shall be called . . . Counsellor." But when the real battles of life begin, and we feel the encroachments of sin, and begin to fear, after many bitter experiences, that the contest is too great for us, then what a blessing to feel the hand that is not shortened that it cannot save; to grow into the use of a power so sure besides our own; to gain little by little through that power true freedom of soul!

And something more: If life is advancing in a truly spiritual way, its experiences will deepen; the temptations become more subtle and less palpable; ay, take the form, sometimes, simply of heart-weariness, of pain of mind, with no assignable outward cause. Such states are beyond the touch of human hands; are not seen by our own eyes. And for that very reason one feels helpless in such suffering. But some day we may be able to look back, and recognize these two facts: (1) These states of dejection and of pain, for which we could find no apparent cause, were not because of any sickness of the body, but resulted from assaults made upon our spiritual life. (2) And another truth we shall learn: when in such states, and the soul was faint, the power of the Lord's life came and gently brought us out of them; protected us with His life; fought for us.

And by such rescuings, and by the power offered at every turn with which to resist evil and keep true, we shall know then, better even than we can now know by any force of argument, that the Lord is spiritually present with men; and that that presence, because so constant, so sure in its might, so unfailing in its mercy and forgiveness, is divine, — the very presence of God.

THE LORD AS THE EVERLASTING FATHER.

O Love! O Life! our faith and sight
  Thy presence maketh one;
As through transfigured clouds of white
  We trace the noonday sun, —

So, to our mortal eyes subdued,
  Flesh-veiled, but not concealed,
We know in Thee the Fatherhood
  And heart of God revealed.
Whittier.

The Lord as the Everlasting Father.

✠

"*And His name shall be called . . . the everlasting Father.*"

✠

HOW often our Saviour, when He revealed Himself in the flesh, spoke of the Father! No other name is so often on His lips. More than one hundred and fifty times the evangelists caught that divine name in so much of the conversations and prayers as they have set down in our four Gospels. And very wonderful it is to trace, not so much how often, as in what way, under what circumstances, this word "Father" was used. What is the first exclamation that escapes His lips, of which we have any record? "Wist ye not that I must be about my Father's business?" Divine work waiting for those eager hands! Divine rescuings and consolations already looked forward to with eagerness by One who should some day be saying: "I am come to seek and to save that which was lost." Such work was divine. To Himself, to men on the earth, it should appear as divine. They praised Him for His gracious words; but He told them that He spoke not from Himself but from the Father. They praised Him for His works. "He hath done all things well," they cried; "He maketh both the deaf to hear and the dumb to speak." But He told them: "The Father that dwelleth in Me, He doeth the works." All the kindly acts, all the sacrifices that were being made for them, — the seeking and finding and bringing home once more, — He would not let them think of all this as though it were simply the result of human benevolence. Let them know that all this ·desire and effort to redeem and save them was the Divine desire. "I came not to do mine own will; but the will of Him that sent me." For here was a fact for them to learn as they had never learned it before: God is a God of love. He sustains the same relation to them that a good father would to his children, only far more perfectly and unfailingly. It was written in their own sacred books, "Like as a Father pitieth His children, so the Lord pitieth them that fear Him." And yet their chief thought of Him had been that He was a great Ruler; severe in judgment; easily offended; relentless in His punishments. But He who declared that He had come forth from God, and whose purpose it was to make Him manifest, did not speak of Him as a dread monarch, but kept referring to the Father. They need not be afraid of Him: "I say not unto you that I will pray the Father for you; for the Father himself loveth you." Let them enter into their closets, and when they have shut the door, pray to this Father in secret. Yea, let the first words of their petitions be: "Our Father." "And this is the Father's will," He said, "that of all which He hath given Me, I should lose nothing, but should raise it up again at the last day." Yes, and this Divine desire that nothing might be lost, extends to the least of God's children; for He said, "It is not the will of your Father who is in heaven that one of these little ones should perish." With steadfast love "their angels" — that is, the children's angels — "behold the face of their Father in heaven." And all men, if they learn the law of love, shall be the children of this Father who is in heaven; for He, in His love, maketh His sun to rise on the evil and on the good, and sendeth rain on the just and on the unjust. Let them, therefore, strive to be perfect, even as their Father in heaven is perfect. Let them feel sure of His loving care. Not one sparrow shall fall without the Father. The Father knows what things we have need of before we ask Him. If we forgive, the heavenly Father will surely forgive us. " Be ye merciful as your Father also is merciful." " Fear not, little flock ; for it is your Father's good pleasure to give you the Kingdom."

How wonderful all these sayings are! So simple, and yet so all-revealing! If we could only forget the theological controversies which, we might almost say, have been hammered out of such passages ; if we could but keep our minds free of the thought of separate persons, and come back to this great truth, which the Lord kept impressing upon men's hearts, that however else they might think of the Divine Being, essentially God is a Father; and that this Divine Father, in all His thoughts " which are to us ward," in every heart-throb, is Love!

And then if we could feel that the Lord, in word, in deed, was manifesting that Father; was acting from and embodying that love which is the essence of the Divine Fatherhood! From that love, in ever-increasing fulness, He acted. "In His love and in His pity He redeemed them." From that fatherly desire to guide and save, He spoke and taught. Every errand of mercy on which He went forth, whether to heal, to befriend, to forgive, was prompted by this same undying love. Well might He say, "I came forth from the Father." He never went forth from any mere purpose of His own. And when His work was done, no matter whether He had been resisted, or mocked, or abused, He always came back to this same state of loving solicitude; never took refuge in thoughts or feelings of self-vindication or retribution. "I go to my Father." And it was this going and returning in perfect love, that kept bringing this fatherly or Divine Love in ever-increasing fulness into every act, thought, wish; so that He could eventually say, "I and the Father are one." No wonder He said in sad reproach to Philip, who asked, "Show us the Father," "Have I been so long time with you, and yet hast thou not known Me, Philip!" Through all the days of their discipleship, had He not been speaking, purposing, coming and going in this spirit of fatherly love? Did He not embody that love? Did it not possess and inspire every least thing of His life? Essentially then, had they not seen the Father?

Oh, it seems unspeakably beautiful, this constant reference of our Saviour to the Divine Fatherhood in His work, the moment we free our minds from the perplexing thoughts of separate beings or personalities, and allow to the Lord's words a more spiritual quality and intention. We make awkward literalisms of

His words; when yet His very words were "spirit and life." His words are not used at random. Neither are they used in that stiff, literal way in which we use them. They are sensitive with meaning. This is equally true of His use of names. Did He not see a good reason for naming Simon, "Cephas" or Peter, a stone? When He would speak of the sufferings of His Humanity, His rejection, persecution, what term does He use? It is "the Son of Man" that hath not where to lay His head! It is "the Son of Man" that goeth forth as was determined. It is the "Son of Man" that is to be betrayed. It is the "Son of Man" that must be lifted up, even as Moses lifted up the serpent in the wilderness. Why, the multitudes were quicker than we to catch these spiritual differences. If they came to question Him about some truth, they addressed Him as "Rabbi." When their thoughts were about His Messianic office, they speak either of the "Messiah" or "the Christ." When, in His saving work, He is removing evil, the very devils call Him "Jesus" (so named because He should save His people from their sins). When, by means of the Truth, He is carrying out the purposes of the Divine Love, He speaks ever of "the Son." But when He would speak of the Love itself, how it is the ever-active and controlling purpose or desire from which He is living, then that word "Father" is on His lips.

Think of but one Divine Being, whose life is Love and Wisdom going forth into infinite forms and varieties of use. Think of the Humanity of the Lord, as the special instrument by means of which the Divine Love and Wisdom might come down and become established in all the successive planes or degrees of angelic and human life, make them Divine in Himself, and through them flow forth with a new power of saving help. And then, in this marvellous process, in this amazing work of redemption and salvation, think of the different states through which the Lord passed, the different relationships which He sustained to men, as expressed by the various names which are employed. There is then no confusion of persons; but the most wonderful, the most thrilling spiritual delineation of what we may dare to call the story of the Divine Life in its descent to man through the Humanity of Jesus Christ; of the combats of truth, of the appealings of love, of the guidings of wisdom, of joy in salvation, of pain and patience in being despised and rejected. Why, in all that the world has to tell us, whether of the marvellous in science, the heroic in history, the beautiful in art, there is nothing that begins to compare with the marvellous, the heroic, the beautiful, which as yet only faintly dawn upon us out of this story of the Divine Life, in its accommodations, its labors, its rejections, its victories among men. And what could be of more thrilling interest in our religious studies, than to be able to read that story with some perception and appreciation of the different delicate meanings and phases of it; to see, for instance, that when the term "Son of Man" is used, the experiences of suffering in the Lord's Humanity are being treated of; that when "Jesus" is spoken of, it is the Lord in His efforts to save, that is the theme, — efforts which men may so resist, as in mockery, yet sad truthfulness, to place this word "Jesus" over a crucified Saviour, — that when "the Christ" is spoken of, it is the Divine Truth trying to gain spiritual supremacy for us; that when "the Father" is mentioned, it is the Divine Love, unwavering, unchangeable, merciful, forgiving, that shows itself for our loving!

I would liken this use of the Divine names to the use of what are known as *Leitmotifs*, which have been made famous through Wagner's development of them in his music-dramas. Not only is there for every one of the *dramatis personae*, a *motif* or musical theme, but in many cases the changing moods, passions, episodes of the several characters, whether of love, of combat, of fear, of victory, are also expressed by their special musical phrases. Very brief and simple these *motifs* often are; and yet no matter when they recur, through what dissonance of sound they are heard, they carry with them and keep bringing back to the hearer, the story, the eventful mood or episode, with which they are associated. And so, to one knowing these themes, this music, as in the "Tetralogy," is vocal with ideas. It may recount incidents without words; as in the dirge following *Siegfried's* death, in which by the recurrence of the *motifs* already made familiar, all the virtues and the life-episodes of the dead — the adventures, the fearlessness, the love-life,

— are rehearsed in this noble musical epitome, with an eloquence and expressiveness which the orator could scarcely hope to equal.

In somewhat the same way, as it seems to me, the several Divine names, as we come to understand and make ourselves familiar with them, may be as so many *motifs* employed in celebrating the story of the Christ-life in humanity. Think how wonderful this would be. Nay, think how wonderful it *is;* for have we not in part seen it to be so? " Wonderful," " Counsellor," " Mighty God," — have we not recognized in these appellations distinct phases of the Lord's life in the world, and more especially in the spiritual life of men? "Son of Man," "Son of God," " Jesus," " the Christ," — can we not already see that these terms are expressive of different qualities, and we might almost say, episodes in the life of our Lord? And then this term " Father," — can we fail to see that it is expressive of Divine Love from which the Lord lived, taught, acted?

See, then, what is involved in this promise: "His name shall be called . . . the everlasting Father." When can the Lord, in the development of His life in us, be called our Father? He is to us "the Wonderful," when, as the God-with-us, He draws out our wonder, our reverence. He is for us "the Counsellor," when we feel that He is the living embodiment of the Divine Truth, and we go to Him in faith with our questions concerning eternal life. He is for us "the Mighty God," when through Him we gain power over our evils. He is for us "the everlasting Father," when we come to act from His love. When a man can truly say, "I delight to do Thy will, O my God; yea, thy law is within my heart," for him the promise is come true: the Lord is become "the everlasting Father."

Need it be said that this is not accomplished at once? Is it necessary to say, that before we can feel this intimate and altogether loving relationship, we must first reverence, and then be instructed of Him, and then carry on a long and oftentimes discouraging struggle against the evils of our nature? Not that we would make this state seem hard of attainment. And yet we would rightly estimate it. We would, if possible, think of it and look forward to it as no light or sentimental blessing. Very many, let us hope, are living their lives in the general desire to do what is right. But in this, much of what we do is actuated by a sense of *duty*. There may be even lower motives by which we are sometimes actuated, such as the desire for reward, the fear of appearing ill, of doing ourselves injury. In this first state of the regenerating life, truth has to take the lead; and the will comes dragging on behind. It is "I must *try* to do this," or "I *ought* to do that." It is duty, duty, duty, all the time; checking ourselves here, spurring ourselves there. It is facing evils, reluctantly turning from vanities, silencing doubts, quelling inward mutinies. It is being happy one day, discouraged another. It is being trustful one hour, and anxious and faithless the next. It is crying in a sudden moment of enthusiasm: "Lord, I will follow thee both to prison and to death;" and then again, when faith is cold, and the fires of self-love are blazing, saying to our tormentors, "I know not the man!"

And is this the all of religion? Are we summoned to enter the way of Truth only that we may have to battle, and keep compelling ourselves, and be almost haunted by this spirit of Duty? When man goes forth like Elijah to stand upon the mount before the Lord, is it only wind, and earthquake, and fire that shall sweep, and rumble, and kindle about him? Is there no release from these wild gusts of temptations, these tremblings, and burnings of the spirit? Is there no silence; no still voice to speak to the troubled heart, and make it feel the nearness and the friendliness of God?

Oh, the innumerable multitude on which the eyes of the loved disciple rested, arrayed in white, and palms in their hands, of whom the angel said: "These are they which have come out of great tribulation. . . . And they hunger no more, neither thirst any more; neither shall the sun light on them, nor any heat." There comes an end to these self-compulsions. For those who will be faithful unto the end, the "Go" in religion shall change to "Come!" This is a real change; a change in man's nature. First, Truth must lead the way, and the man with his sluggish or rebellious will must try to follow. It is of this state that we know most now. But we are assured that there is another state, — and it is sure to follow, if we do not try to avoid the first, — in which love takes the first part. There is a reversal. Love flows into thought, impels it, inspires it. What was before a duty is now a delight. What before required effort is now a desire. In this history of religion, which every man lives out for himself, the Lord is more than a wonder, exciting his reverence; more than a Counsellor, teaching him the way of life; more, even, than a mighty God, helping him to overcome his evils. In this new state of harmony and delight for what Divine Love desires, the Lord assumes a new relationship, — that of a Father. There is mutual love; mutual joy. And yet I realize how powerless words are to set forth a state so blessed. For "eye hath not seen, nor ear heard, neither have entered into the heart of man, the things which God hath prepared for them that love Him."

Only it is everything to know that such a state is possible; nay, that such a state shall certainly be if we persist in the life of struggle and duty which is the present experience of most of us. It is everything to know, that by persistent faithfulness one's life shall come into such harmony with the Divine Life, as to insure a relationship as near, as friendly, as mutual, as that of father and son.

The difference in these states and relationships seems to me to be beautifully expressed by the two Sacraments, which stand, the one at the beginning, the other at the close of the Lord's ministry. In Baptism there is the sign of a regenerating work to be accomplished. The Lord is to be acknowledged and followed; evils are to be removed. Whether it be the brow of the babe or of the man that receives the sign of the cross, the symbol expresses the same hope. Seen in heaven, seen by men on the earth, the sacrament testifies that the person baptized should become the Lord's faithful follower, and should look to Him for help in removing evil. Such was the sacrament which, at the very beginning of the Lord's ministry, His disciples were permitted to administer in His name.

But see how different is the sacrament which is instituted on the last night of that loving ministry. These men, who at first followed more in awe than in love, who have been His almost constant companions, are reclining with Him about a table from which they have eaten the Passover meal. For three years they have been taught by Him; they have had an experience of His love; they have, in a measure, shared His sorrows and joys. And now for the last time on earth they are gathered together. No crowds are about to disturb the quiet of that meeting and that parting. In an upper room, away from "the strife of tongues," away, it must almost have seemed to them, from earth itself, they lingered in each other's companionship. One strangely touching act of loving service He had performed, which must have inwardly rebuked the pride which had led them to strive for the best seats, and brought them into a state of humility. For quietly, from one to the other, not even omitting Iscariot, girded with a towel, and bearing a basin of water, He washed the feet of His followers. And when He had taken His place again, with the loved disciple resting His head upon His breast, Judas having gone forth, as they reclined there, a sorrowful tenderness drawing them spiritually near together, He drew from the food before Him the two simplest elements, — some bread and a chalice of wine. And to His "little children," as He called them that night, He distributed with words of blessing the bread and the wine, and bade them in the days that were coming to celebrate this loving meal in remembrance of Him. We know not with what looks of anxious, tender love these men met His eyes, as one by one the bits of bread and the chalice found their way from His hands to theirs. But one thing we cannot miss seeing: into what a loving and tender friendship the discipleship of these rude, simple-hearted men had grown! And the Last Supper, to those who still partake of it in love, shall always express that near and dear relationship, which "with desire" the Lord looks forward to; and which, when it is once established, brings joy and calm. To receive from Him in love and faith pure affections and thoughts, as the disciples received the symbols of His Body and Blood; to be fed at His table, is to know Him not as a distant God but as a Father, — the "Father Everlasting." For that state, when once established, shall not be destroyed. It shall endure; and the joy of it shall extend into eternity.

Do we, then, complain of present struggles? Do we falter in the strife? Do we feel held down to the world and its life?

> " What is the world? It is a waiting place
> Where men put on their robes for that above.
> What is the new world? 'T is a Father's face
> Beholden of His sons, — the face of love."

THE LORD AS THE PRINCE OF PEACE.

PEACE beginning to be
Deep as the sleep of the sea
When the stars their faces glass
In its blue tranquillity:
Hearts of men upon earth,
Never once still from their birth,
To rest as the wild waters rest
With the colors of heaven on their breast!

Love which is sunlight of peace,
Age by age to increase
Till anger and hatred are dead,
And sorrow and death shall cease:
"Peace on earth and good-will."
Souls that are gentle and still
Hear the first music of this
Far-off, infinite bliss!

EDWIN ARNOLD.

The Lord as the Prince of Peace.

✠

"And His Name shall be called . . . the Prince of Peace."

✠

OF the names which we have considered as rightly belonging to the Child and Son, upon whose shoulder, it was declared in prophecy, the government should some day rest, names which, I trust we have come to see, disclose the different relationships which the Lord successively sustains to every man who suffers himself to be divinely led; is there one that is more beautiful, more appealing than this last title of all? The Prince of Peace! How perfectly this seems to describe that wonderful blending of majesty and gentleness, of power and love, of energy and calm, which give one such a sense of completeness, of strength, of absolute self-control in this perfect life of all! "I am meek and lowly in heart," He said. Would any of us gainsay that? No service so homely but He would perform it; no house so humble but He would enter it; no obligation so small but He would fulfil it. And yet something in that presence made men feel there was nothing abject in this meekness. "Lord, I am not worthy that Thou shouldst come under my roof," exclaimed the centurion to his would-be guest. Why does yonder man kneel to Him in the boat and cry, "Depart from me, for I am a sinful man, O Lord"? And why, on the night of the Last Supper, does that same man shrink as His Master kneels to wash his feet, and exclaim, "Lord, Thou shalt never wash my feet"? Why do these angry men of Nazareth, who had led Him to the brow of the hill with the intention of casting Him down headlong, fall back suddenly, and allow Him to pass through their midst unhindered and unharmed? Why do these demoniacs fall at His feet wallowing and foaming, as if His very presence was more than they could bear? Why does the mob, who have come out, as if against some thief, with lights and weapons, fall to the ground as He quietly advances to them and says, "I am He"?

Oh, there was no lack of strength, nor of majesty! Hero, Prince, King, the sacred books had called Him. And the children of Israel, seizing upon such prophecies, thought He would come and marshal them to victory; that He would visibly restore the throne of their father David. And when they saw Him riding into Jerusalem one day, with a multitude about Him, they thought that He had come to be their King, and that the Kingdom of God would suddenly appear. And so, in an ecstasy of joy, they covered the road with fronds of the palm, and with their garments; they waved palm-branches as to a mighty conqueror; and a great shout went up, "Hosanna to the Son of David!" "Blessed is the King of Israel that cometh in the name of the Lord!"

They were right in saluting Him so. Had not the prophet said long ago, —

> "Rejoice greatly, O daughter of Zion;
> Shout, O daughter of Jerusalem.
> Behold thy King cometh unto thee:
> He is just and having salvation;
> Lowly, and riding upon an ass;
> And upon a colt, the foal of an ass."

And in that Kingdom which He declared to be His, but which is "not from hence," did not the Seer of Patmos hear this song go reverberating through the opened heavens: —

> "Worthy is the Lamb that was slain
>   To receive power, and riches, and wisdom,
> And strength, and honor, and glory, and blessing."

The Lord came to establish Himself in power among men; to be their deliverer from a bondage far worse than that of Rome; to make bare His holy arm, and fight for them against the assaults of evil power; to be a Prince, around whose banner they might flock. But did we ever think what it cost the Lord to be a Prince, not of armed hosts, but of *Peace?* To rule, not by might, nor by power, but by the Spirit? Have we ever thought how, in that great work of Redemption which He came to accomplish, the seeming hopelessness of triumphing through Love, through Truth, must sometimes have been borne in upon Him? To be a Prince, not through any use of forces and powers such as fire men's enthusiasm and admiration, but by spiritual conquests which we all are so apt to shun! To be a Prince, not of this world, nor through the might of this world, but of Peace!

See! In that mysterious waiting-time, which was spent in the wilderness, before fully entering upon the outward work of His ministry, there was unfolded a view of dominion and of spreading empires which were intended as a temptation. A spirit of darkness — by what magic it matters not — summoned, as in a vision, the kingdoms of the world. Province after province, empire after empire rose under his touch, until the glory of earth seemed spread out before them. And yet the spirit of evil must have known how gross and cheap dominion of this kind would appear to the Son of Man. What to Him was earthly dominion? What though the kingdoms of this world and the glory of them lay at His feet? Could He not have claimed the right to say, in words which had been written to declare the power of the advent of God-Messiah, "If I were hungry, I would not tell thee: for the world is Mine and the fulness thereof." Why then this vision? Can we doubt it? To make that kingdom of Truth and Love, which He has come to establish among men, and which all hell would try to shatter, appear unreal; to make its establishment seem impossible, except by means of that power and cunning which the tempter only too well personified.

At every step one can feel the cunning of this suggestion. Did not the people come searching for Him one day, determined to take Him by force, if necessary, and make Him their King? Did not two of His disciples beg that they might invoke the lightning to punish those who drove Him from their doors? Did not Simon Peter, who once before had tried to hold Him back from coming persecution, press forward to His side as He stood there in Gethsemane, waiting for the mob to take Him, and whisper eagerly, "Lord, shall we smite with the sword?" And as He hung on the cross, must not this same apparent need of force, and the victory that might be won by it, have come to Him through that cruel taunt which they flung at Him: "If He be the King of Israel, let Him now come down from the cross, and we will believe Him." One miracle, put forth for His own safety, and they might believe!

Is there not something wonderfully pathetic in this constant refusal to turn away, for so much as one moment, from that Kingdom of the Spirit wherein worldliness and mere force can have no place. Beyond the reach of a "lo! here," or "lo! there," it was already springing up in a few faithful hearts. It was promised to "the poor in spirit;" it was held out to those " who are persecuted for righteousness sake;" it is the home of children, and of all who are humble and teachable as children, "for of such," said its founder, "is the Kingdom of Heaven." The kingdoms of this world might rise, or they might fall; but this "Kingdom of God," lying vast, silent, hidden in humble and contrite hearts, would be an "everlasting Kingdom," and the dominion of its King would endure "throughout all generations."

No weak, no merely sentimental title that, — Prince of Peace! It was not won without struggle and pain. And it tells of the unconquerableness of a power, which we, accustomed to a lower rule, where force is met with force, where money and rank seem to have such might, need to cling to and believe in. Do we fret ourselves because of evil doers; and are we sometimes envious against the workers of iniquity? Do we see evil men prospering, and bringing wicked devices to pass? Have we sometimes seen the wicked in great power, and spreading himself like a green bay-tree; while the righteous apparently fail?

When thoughts and fears like these oppress;

when this world's life, with its seeming power and pressure and tremendousness appears fairly to crowd out and dwarf that Kingdom of the Spirit which the Prince of Peace came to make supreme, I know of nothing more reassuring than to turn in thought to that scene in the Judgment Hall, with its two figures who stand facing each other. One is a proud, cruel, truculent ruler, watchful only of Rome's power, absolutely indifferent to all questions of a spiritual nature, the very personification of world-might: the other, the very embodiment of unworldliness, no symbols of wealth or power upon Him, standing there in perfect calmness and simplicity, and treating His would-be judge with gentle courtesy. It is a sight not to be forgotten! The "prince of this world" facing, questioning, eying, the Prince of Peace! The power of earth trying to pass judgment upon the power of holiness! Human might measuring itself against eternal

Truth and Love! We all know how uneasy, and then anxious, and then frightened grew this man, who began by declaring, "Knowest Thou not that I have power to crucify Thee, and I have power to release Thee?" We all know how he tried to escape his responsibility; the expedients he resorted to, — now sending Him to Herod, now offering to chastise Him, now trying to turn over Barabbas instead. And we all know, too, how quiet and reposeful was the bearing of Him whom Pilate tried to judge; how few and simple were the words which He spoke, and in which He affirmed His Kingship.

And this is the truth, the lesson of it all to which we should cling: There came to Pontius Pilate a vision of strength, of royalty and grace, before which all human or earthly conceptions and standards utterly broke down. And he gained it through One, who, to the eye that could look upon His form and visage, appeared friendless, spent, weary. He saw patience, fearlessness, and a certain repose that betokened untold strength, in One who could not be frightened, nor angered, nor crushed. The more they mocked Him, the surer seemed His majesty. The more they did violence, the greater the strength of spirit. The more they sought to destroy Him, the more surely and serenely did He seem to hold His Kingship.

It was the spiritual, the eternal, proving its might over the natural and temporal. Before this absolute peacefulness of soul, human authority lost its boastfulness and courage. Little the Lord said to Pilate; did not argue with him; did not threaten him. For the most part He remained silent. Not because he hated Pilate; but because Pilate needed nothing so much as the sight of One, who, apparently weak and dependent on the governor's clemency, stood calm and strong through a power of which Pilate knew nothing. He does not assail the Kingdom of the Cæsars; He simply reveals another that is higher, and against which the powers of the world might beat in vain.

To one who has had some experience in trying to be governed by spiritual, rather than by natural motives; who knows their difference, in what opposite directions they tend; who knows, too, that with the best of intentions, sometimes, even after we have resolved to act from a high principle, something of self, some fear, some thought of self-interest or advantage will spring up in one's path and demand to be heard, — to such an one, it must ever remain a subject of the deepest wonder and reverence, that every thought or feeling in the Humanity of our Lord, that might look to self or the world, was entirely subjugated; every word, desire, deed, directed absolutely to divine ends.

And when, through the Gospel story, we see Him come down from the mountain, where He had been praying, and, in the strength of a renewed consciousness of the Divine Presence which He had thus gained, walk out upon the angry sea; or when we read of His coming to Jerusalem riding upon an ass, and upon a colt the foal of an ass, while the people hailed Him as King; then through scenes like these, the truth seems to gain form and reality; the truth that the Lord gained absolute power over every form of evil; placed it, as it were, under His feet; and that all the lower powers and faculties, whether of the natural mind or physical body, — the very powers and faculties which in us are apt to assert themselves as masters, — were brought into complete subjection to those which were higher. And as we gain a view of that fact in our Lord's life, then we can begin to have some appreciation of what He intended by the exclamation: "I have overcome the world!" The world! The thoughts, the loves, the ways, that belong to the world; all its fears, its harshness, its retaliations, its love of power, of ease, of approbation; this world, in which we are now battling, a corner of which we should be glad to really subdue; He could say of it, "I have overcome the world!" Say it; and manifest it; not simply by symbolic acts such as we just spoke of, but in actual experiences of pain. So that when Judas pressed his lips against His cheek, He spake only in grief; when false witnesses accused Him, He was dumb with silence; when the coward soldiers buffeted and spit upon Him, there was nothing like anger; and when they crucified Him, there were no imprecations, but a prayer for their forgiveness.

We might suppose that this was through a supreme effort of self-control; that by a mighty effort of the will, the lips were not permitted to utter the words of remonstrance and denial and accusation that were ready to be spoken. But I believe there was a fact much more wonderful than that. I believe that all those thoughts and feelings, which in us would have taken arms, and risen in rebellion, were being absolutely and forever subdued and cast forth; that our Lord so entirely overcame this earthly nature, with its thoughts and desires, that though men dragged Him through the streets, scourged Him, nailed Him to a cross, jeered at Him, they could not stir up a harsh thought nor an unkind feeling. In other words, this spiritual self-conquest was so complete, the Divine came down so fully into these lower planes of life, that inwardly there was a calm and a peace which nothing could destroy.

And we may think of this somewhat in this way: Far back in the Lord's human life, because of the difference in its origin and the far greater richness of that primitive mind which was Divinely begotten, He was conscious of a feeling of intense love. Whence that love was, whence that nameless delight, that intense yearning, the little Christ-Child did not at first clearly know. But we may think of Him as gradually becoming conscious of it; and then gradually realizing that He alone had it. We may think of Him as gently learning, through the opened Scriptures, whence this love was, and why He had it, and how it was to become His very life. And when the truth of His real mission had grown bright before Him, then how beautiful it is to think of Him as planning to bring all that He could of this loving power to others, to bring them new life, — the life of His spirit. Not at once could He do this; nor could He give that Spirit in its fulness until every least hindrance in Himself had been removed. "The Holy Spirit was not yet given because that Jesus was not yet glorified." But though not completed until the crucifixion, that work of glorification, of removing everything that looked to evil or was earth-born, and bringing the Divine into union and absolute oneness with the Human, was constantly going on. And as it went on, the Lord experienced more and more in His Humanity the delight of the Divine life. It brought a sense of rest and peace, so perfect, so profound, that He bade all who were weary and heavy laden — as many a time He had been — to come unto Him that He might share it with them, and give them rest. And on the night of the Last Supper, the conflicts so nearly over, as they recline about the table, there is within the sorrow of treachery and the knowledge of approaching trials, a calmness of spirit, a peace, which He would fain share with those who are sadly clinging to Him. "Peace I leave with you," He says to these friends, these companions, these "little children" of His; "*My* peace I give unto you." That sense of perfect rest and love and confidence, that conquest over evil, that freedom from uncharitableness, He would have them have. "Not as the world giveth, give I unto you." No, the world's way is to indulge and satisfy our selfish wants: His way to overcome them, and in their place to experience a calmness of spirit, a free delight in good, which cannot be taken away. And then He is taken from them; but only for "a little while," as He had said. And when He comes before them again, this is His salutation: "Peace be unto you!" "And He breathed on them," say the Gospels, "and said, 'Receive ye the Holy Spirit.'"

And now it only remains for us to ask, How may the Lord be to us a Prince of Peace? We have thought of Him as the Wonderful, when, by the presence of His Divinely-Human life among men, He excites our wonder, our reverence. We have thought of Him as the Counsellor, when, in the confidence that He is the embodiment of the Divine Truth, we go to Him for instruction in the way of life. He is to us "the Mighty God," when through His power we learn to overcome evil. He is for us "the Everlasting Father," when we have an experience of His love, and come to feel a delight in acting from such love. He is to us "the Prince of Peace," when, after His example, having persevered in shunning evils as sin, the lusts arising from the love of self and of the world are gradually removed, and in their place there is received from Him a blessedness of heart and soul. When there is no longer any combat of the false and evil against the good and the true, when there is no spiritual discord or war, then there is contentment, rest, peace.

Far away such a state, as a permanent one, may seem to some of us, who know more of struggle and conflict than this deep calm of soul which cannot be destroyed. And yet it is the sure portion of every faithful follower. Into that state the Lord invites all. "Come unto Me, *all* ye that labor and are heavy laden, and I will give you rest." Not through crying, " Peace ! Peace !" when there is no peace; not through any sickly sentiment, nor morbid state of the feelings, while evil loves are still unsubdued, can we gain that rest of soul. " Take my yoke and learn of Me, . . . and ye shall find rest unto your souls." First, there must be yokes and lessons, — lessons out of this life of Christ our Lord, whose peace came through victory over evil.

Nor let us be disheartened if this greatest of all blessings, the very fruit of all patient, persistent effort, should be the last in coming. Think of the Lord's own experience.

If what was said above is true, He first perceived with a sense of delight the love that was to be given through Him to men, and with quiet, yet eager joy began "to be about (His) Father's business." But before that desire could be fully realized, there was a period of spiritual combat to be undergone, so that Divine Love might be unhindered. The extent of those inward struggles, the depth and intensity of them, who shall tell? But when they were accomplished, when He had "overcome the world," then peace reigned.

Answering to these three stages or spiritual epochs in the Lord's life, there are three periods in a regenerating man's life.

First, he enters upon the life of his religion in a state comparatively of spiritual tranquillity. He looks forward to the blessedness of it with happy, peaceful expectations; something in the same way that the Lord contemplated with joy the bringing forth of the

Divine Love. It is a very tender, a very precious time in a man's life. It is the time when a young man or a young woman may feel moved to make an open acknowledgment of their desire to live a Christian life. On bended knees, confessing their Saviour, receiving the Church's blessing, a young man or young woman virtually says, " Lord, I will follow Thee." Not for the sake of praising such acts would we speak; but rather to dwell for a single moment upon the joy and tenderness of that state in one's life. If, in Divine mercy, we have had it, we may well think of it and keep it as sacred. If any are considering it, or really looking forward to it, let them feel that it is the Lord's own loving desire for them that has awakened what seems to be their desire for better life; and let them honor it, and confirm it, and be inwardly grateful that the true way of life is opening up before them.

And if, following this tranquil joy and expectation, there comes one that is far different, — a state of temptation and conflict, — let them not be surprised nor dismayed. Was it not the Lord's own way? "Wist ye not that I must be about my Father's business?" There was joy as of heaven in that prospect. But what followed? The hour was not yet come. To Nazareth He returned, and for eighteen years His life seemed a life of common labor and trial. "Seemed," I say, because in that very experience of self-denial, in the waiting of those long years, in the inward struggles that must have come to Him as day by day He lived that simple, industrious, self-denying life, He was advancing far along the perfect way. Step by step He advanced; was tempted, assailed, weary oftentimes. "I do cures to-day and to-morrow, and the third day I shall be perfected. Nevertheless I must walk to-day, and to-morrow, and the day following." Oh, the gradual, the almost plodding life of regeneration; that long and seemingly never-ending *second* state, with its difficulties and trials, its struggles and spiritual weariness! Many of us know what it is to say, "I must walk to-day and to-morrow, and the day following!" Always some call for new effort! Always some new state to be attained!

And yet, when we see that this period, this long stretch in life, is orderly; that we cannot expect to stay in that first state of happy expectation, why then there is no cause for discouragement. Let there be the courage to say, "I do cures to-day and to-morrow, and the third day [that third completed state] I shall be perfected." The work will then have been done; the internal strife will have been ended; the yokes will have been borne; the lessons learned. And then comes the promised rest of soul!

Not a mere time of respite, and then the struggle to be taken up again; but a new state of life, a new condition of spiritual existence; evil subdued and removed, and the Lord our Prince of Peace.

So the first state of tranquillity passes into the longer one of combat; and the state of combat, if we remain faithful, leads into endless peace.

. . . . . .

At the close of these studies, we would make the last words a prayer that we may all, each under the Lord's wise and loving guidance, find Him to be to us, in our quest for the Divine Life, in our search for the Truth, in our struggles with evils and adversities, in our desire for good, in our patient waiting for rest from temptation, the Wonderful, the Counsellor, the Mighty God, the Father of Eternity, the Prince of Peace.

"More than one I count my pastures
   As my life-path groweth long;
By their quiet waters straying
   Oft I lay me, and am strong.
And I call each by its giver,
   And the dear names bring to them
Glory as from shining faces
   In some New Jerusalem."

APPENDIX.

APPENDIX.

A.

THE STORY OF THE VIRGIN BIRTH.—ITS AUTHENTICITY.

IT is a delight to believe that the Christ is less a fact of cold theology than ever before. More good is undertaken and done in the name and in the spirit of Him who said, "Follow Me," than at any time since the Christian Church began. But let us not mistake. With all the personal attachment which it seems certain the Christian world feels in its contemplation of the life of the Son of Man, with all its happy enthusiasm for that ideal of charity and unselfish service which He has set before us, nevertheless, the thought with so many — both in and out of the churches — now is, that the virgin birth is hardly to be insisted upon as true; and that for all He was so sinless, so perfect in love, in wisdom, in patient devotion, He yet was sprung from our own race. To account for the story of the virgin birth in the Gospels, it is declared that it grew up "long after" the Lord's death. Says a writer: "These stories about His birth are very late and of no authority. The Jews expected their Messiah to be born in Bethlehem; so, after the people came to believe that Jesus was the Messiah, this belief grew up."

A very plausible explanation, except that, in this case, it utterly ignores the attitude which, both by word and by deed, the Saviour took, and which led to His final condemnation by the church rulers, who accused Him of blasphemy on this ground: "For a good work we stone Thee not; but for blasphemy; and *because that Thou being a man makest Thyself God.*" Furthermore, unless the story of the

Nativity, as given in St. Luke's Gospel, be an addition of a later age, that story could not have grown up "many years" after the Saviour's death; for it is now practically conceded by friend and foe that this third Gospel, together with the Acts, was written by one Luke, a companion of Paul.

It might be claiming too much to declare that the "Ignatian controversy" is settled; but certain it is that very many regard as authentic the martyrdom of Ignatius in Rome, not later than 116 A. D., or on the more generally accepted supposition of a twofold expedition of Trajan against the Parthians, that he perished December 20, 107 A. D. In his Epistle to the Ephesians (I quote from the shorter version), he writes:—

" For our God, Jesus Christ, was, according to the appointment of God, conceived in the womb by Mary, of the seed of David, but by the Holy Ghost. . . . Now the virginity of Mary was hidden from the prince of this world, as was also her offspring, and the death of the Lord; three mysteries of renown which were wrought in silence by God." [1]

Justin Martyr, whose writings are among the most important that have come down from the second century, is known to have lived in the reign of Antoninus Pius; and it is almost equally certain that he suffered martyrdom in the reign of Marcus Aurelius. Approximately, then, the date of his birth may be given as 114 A. D., and that of his death as 165 A. D. This is still near to the apostolic age; and yet in the "Dialogue with Trypho," the genuineness of which is not doubted, appears a full account of the Nativity closely following the narrative as given in St. Matthew.

"And Joseph," writes this Father, "the spouse of Mary, who wished at first to put away his betrothed Mary, supposing her to be pregnant by intercourse

[1] Epistle of Ignatius to the Ephesians, chap. xviii., xix.

with a man, that is, from fornication, was commanded in a vision not to put away his wife; and the angel who appeared to him told him that what is in her womb is of the Holy Ghost. Then he was afraid, and did not put her away; but on the occasion of the first census which was taken in Judea, under Cyrenius, he went up from Nazareth, where he lived, to Bethlehem, to which he belonged, to be enrolled; for his family was of the tribe of Judah, which then inhabited that region."

And yet it is the spiritual side of the Incarnation, its meaning, its influence, its relation to us personally, that we are most desirous to understand, and which it has been the primary object of this book to set forth.

B.

(See Page 41.)

A LAW OF CREATION AS APPLIED TO THE MIRACULOUS CONCEPTION.

MAN is essentially a spiritual being. In the very form of his creation, that which essentially is the man, which loves, thinks, makes plans and efforts for useful life, is spiritual. It certainly is not material. And doubtless very much of our perplexity and unbelief would utterly disappear, if we could break away from the materialism in which our bodily senses try to hold us, and realize that there are forces and substances within matter higher than matter, apart from matter, and, above all, more enduring than matter. Thought, love, are real things. What is there more real, more enduring? They make up the real things of our life and character. A man's character is not his body. It is not even of it. The body may be maimed, blind, deaf, lame. It may become injured; it may die. But all the time, surely, there is a something, a spiritual nature or organism, which exercises thought, love, and, whether for good or ill, has a general directing power over the physical body, which it tries to use for the carrying out of its purposes. Because we can see and handle material things, we make them first; give them the palm, so to say, for reality. But science is fast doing us a good service by showing us that even in this outward realm of nature there are forces and substances invisible to the naked eye. And what is more, these inner forces and substances of nature prove to be more highly organized, more charged with life and energy, than the things which come within our sight and under our touch. Moreover, they are primary. They are first, and exercise a directing power. Why limit the law to natural things? Here is nature's testimony that the kingdom of God and His righteousness is indeed first. First the invisible, the internal, the spiritual; then the visible, the external, the material.

For instance, you speak a sentence. There is a succession of sounds; a birth, as it were, of words. And what was the law by which they were created? Clearly, this descent of inmosts into outmosts; first a feeling or intention; then that intention clothing itself in distinct thought; and then the thought articulating itself by means of natural speech. The same is true of every free and conscious act. And in agreement with this law we are not surprised with Swedenborg's[1] declaration, that the seed of man

---

[1] For some, the remark will appear unnecessary, but the author desires to state that the doctrine of the Son of Man which he has tried to set forth in these pages, is stated in its fulness in the theological writings of Swedenborg, to whom the entire Scriptures were a revelation of the Divinity of the Lord Jesus Christ.

is of spiritual origin, clothed upon by natural substances for the sake of conveyance.

Turn now to the words of the angel as set down in the Gospel: "That which is conceived in her is of the Holy Ghost." We are prepared to think of this as something wholly spiritual. We are prepared to think of it as the initiament used in the formation of the Lord's Humanity. Like the initiament in man, it is composed of the substances of the heavenly world, for it is purely spiritual. And the "miraculous" part of this conception would be, that instead of being derived from man as a father, it is from the Divine; and through the chosen instrumentality of her who was hailed as blessed among women, this inmost form of human life, containing within itself divine possibilities, became clothed in a natural body, and in the silent, mysterious way, which is the way of all birth, was born into the world.

C.

THE PERSON OF THE SON OF MAN IN THE LIGHT OF HIS OWN TESTIMONY.

IT is impressive to note in the Gospels how careful the Lord was that men's reverence for Him should not simply be hero-worship; for the Saviour, even in the days when He was crucified, was not without His admirers. They thronged about Him as He entered Jerusalem, and made the city ring with their Hosannas. They followed Him from village to village; and sometimes, when He withdrew to secluded places that He and His disciples might gain a little needed rest, the people, learning where He was, would come to Him by thousands. And well they might; for He not only healed their sick, but He talked to them as no scribe could do of "the kingdom of heaven," and presented to them a religion of love, of personal kindness and forgiveness, of spiritual equality, of unselfish service, such as was new indeed. And all this excited not only the greatest curiosity and wonder, but the greatest personal enthusiasm. Bright with cunning, the Pharisees tried to explain His miracles by ascribing them to Satanic power; but the people quickly replied, "He is a good man," and some went much further, and said, "He must be a prophet;" whilst others asked point blank whether the expected Messiah Himself could excel His works of miracle and love. So there was much enthusiasm and admiration among a certain class. They would wait for an opportunity to touch the hem of His robe; they would bring their sick and lay them in the streets where it was thought He would pass by. Many of them claimed to be His disciples, and went about with Him, and sometimes undertook to do works like Him.

And now the thought comes, what would all this mean if the Lord were simply man? If He were simply man, was it right for men to give, or for Him to receive worship? Was it right for Peter to proclaim Him the Christ, the Son of God Most High? Was it right for the Samaritan leper to turn back in the fulness of his gratitude and worship Him? When John the Evangelist, awed by the vision of the spiritual world and its wonders, fell at the feet of his angel guide, and would have worshipped him, the angel restrained him and said, "See thou do it not; . . . worship God." Was it best, then, that the Saviour should be worshipped if He were only a man, or if the people had no higher thought of Him than that He was a man? "Why callest thou Me good?" He asked of the rich young ruler who came and knelt to Him; "there is but one good: that is God." And unless the young man felt that he was appealing to the Divine in Him, the Lord, it is plain, wished him to see that worship offered to one who was thought of only as a rabbi was not right.

And the moment we begin to examine this point, we find the Gospels rich in testimony of two facts: —

1. The Lord presented Himself as being essential to man's spiritual life. He is the Bread that cometh down from heaven that men may eat thereof and not die. "Without Me ye can do nothing." "Abide in Me, and I in you; as the branch cannot bear fruit of itself, except it abide in the Vine, no more can ye, except ye abide in Me." "I am the Way, the Truth, and the Life." "Come unto Me, all ye that labor and are heavy laden, and I will give you rest."

2. The Lord emphasized at every turn, that He spoke, lived, and acted from the Divine in Himself, and not from Himself apart from the Divine. "The words that I speak unto you, I

speak not of myself." "My doctrine is not mine; but His that sent Me." "I can of Mine own self do nothing." The Lord is telling us that the wisdom and the power in Him are not, as men are fond of saying, the result of any natural development; they are, rather, the very Divine wisdom and power of love received and manifested by Him.

In this thought of the Divine character of all that the Lord did and said, the early Christians found strength and comfort. Men did believe that life, comfort, saving help, came from the risen Lord. Simple and childlike that faith was, if the annalists of the early Church can be believed. They did not formulate it for a time into theological "articles" of belief. They might not have been able to do so. They were content to believe and feel that the Lord was very near to them; that He was the Saviour so long promised, Israel's consolation, the world's hope; and, as Paul expressed it, that in Him dwelleth all the fulness of the Godhead bodily.

We conclude, then, that no amount of critical knowledge can remove these two facts : —

1. That, on the testimony of the Gospels, that Saviour believed that the Divine was in Him; that He lived, spoke, and acted from that Divine; and that because of the fulness of the Divine in Him, He could assume powers and relationships impossible to men on the earth; and,

2. That His apostles and the early converts believed these things with all their hearts, and looked to Him as having all power in heaven and on earth.

D.

A VENERABLE AND REMARKABLE WITNESS.

WITHOUT overlooking the value of the most earnest critical investigations which attempt to determine the character and rightful position of the Son of Man, we believe there is a kind of testimony which the Lord Himself indicated, but which is too often overlooked.

We will think of Him as He stood there in the synagogue of Nazareth, the people of the little town amid whom He had quietly lived gathered that day to hear Him; a hush of expectation falling upon them as He unwound the roll of the book of the prophet Isaiah. And when He had found the place for which He was looking, quietly, we may believe, and in a tone of yearning tenderness, He read the beautiful old prophecy, "The Spirit of Jehovah is upon Me, because He hath anointed Me to preach the gospel to the poor; He hath sent Me to heal the broken-hearted, to preach deliverance to the captives, and recovering of sight to the blind, to set at liberty them that are bruised, to preach the acceptable year of the Lord." And then he handed back the roll to the attendant; and with their eyes still fixed upon Him, standing there in the old familiar place, He broke the silence with these words: "This day is this Scripture fulfilled in your ears." There in his own town He declared Himself to be the Christ of prophecy. A wild, a blasphemous claim if it were not true. But if true — what?

The Old Testament teems with predictions concerning the Son of Man, — of His work; of His kingdom, of His endless reign. No one denies the existence of these prophecies. They had been lying in the Old Testament Scriptures for years, awaiting fulfilment. What shall we say of them if they should prove to be a foreshadowing of certain events which are of immense importance spiritually to the men of to-day, — and this, too, not by merely general or obscure prefigurations, but by references to specific and even minute particulars? And what light would this throw upon the nature and lawful place in our human life of One whose life should prove to have fulfilled the predictions, both in general and in particular, made centuries before His advent? We speak not simply of prophecies which outline in general the nature of the promised Deliverer, as that "the Spirit of Jehovah shall rest upon Him, the Spirit of wisdom and understanding, the Spirit of counsel and might, the Spirit of knowledge and of the fear of Jehovah." Beautiful indeed is the description of One of whom it could be said, "Righteousness shall be the girdle of His loins, and faithfulness the girdle of His reins." But what if prophecies centuries old give events, and particulars of those events, which historical criticism has admitted to be entirely credible? How happens it, for instance, that David in the Psalms should describe the crucifixion almost as graphically as the Gospels themselves, — the gall and the vinegar offered for drink, the dividing of the garments, and the casting of lots for the seamless vesture? How comes it that the twenty-second Psalm begins with the very cry which Jesus uttered on the cross, "My God, my God, why hast thou forsaken Me!" or that the railings of the mob should be foreshadowed in every word and gesture, — " All they that see Me laugh Me to scorn; they shoot out the lip, they shake the head, saying, He trusted the Lord that He would deliver Him; let Him deliver Him seeing He delighted in Him!" How comes it that Isaiah should foretell the trial, as though he had been by when Jesus was brought as a lamb to the slaughter, — as though he had seen the stripes laid upon His back, and the blood-stained visage, and the body hanging between thieves, making "His grave with the wicked," and the tomb of the rich man of Arimathea in which the body was laid? Is it said, The writers of the Gospels evidently made their accounts to square with the prophecies? But these are predictions of facts which no fair historical criticism denies. Nor is it an easy matter, according to the laws of historical or literary evidence, to think of the Gospels as a pious fraud palmed off on the early Christians at a time when the memory of the last agony of Jesus was fresh in every heart.

Here, then, is a plain fact: the Old Testament contains prophecy after prophecy which the life of Christ fulfilled. Nor is this all. The Lord repeatedly points to His life as being a fulfilment of Old Testament Scripture, where no prophecy was suspected; as, for example, where He says, "As Moses lifted up the serpent in the wilderness, so must the Son of Man be lifted up." A statement like this, impressive in itself, becomes still more remarkable when placed with the somewhat broader declaration, that, beginning at Moses and all the prophets, He expounded to two of His disciples in all the Scriptures the things concerning Himself. And this in turn becomes strengthened by the further declaration, "These are the words which I spake unto you while I was yet with you, that all things must be fulfilled which were written in the Law of Moses, and in the prophets, and in the Psalms concerning Me."

This kind of testimony, we maintain, has a right to be considered, in every attempt to determine the question of "evidence." And that the Saviour Himself so thought would seem to be evidenced by His charge, "Search the Scriptures, . . . for they are they which testify of Me."

Nor is this testimony of necessity limited to remote references to the Light of Life, nor even to open predictions of His advent, His work and sufferings; since He Himself has shown the existence of an occult meaning within narratives apparently free of any testimony concerning Himself and His redemption. Something of this has long been recognized; but that much more will be disclosed may confidently be expected. Nor shall we be surprised to find that portions seemingly unimportant to us now, bear this same character.

The building of the temple, for instance; of how little value that appears to be to us in our present life! "But He spake of the temple of His body." And what if that snow-white temple, standing upon Mount Moriah, should prove to be a symbol of our Lord's Humanity. What a new meaning would be imparted to all the particulars connected with it! How expressive the fact, that while it was a-building there was heard within it no sound of axe or hammer! Noiselessly it grew. Stone after stone, column after column, found their place, until at last it stood forth in all its white beauty. And then we think of those silent years in Nazareth. All we know is what the Gospels tell us : " And the child grew in wisdom, and stature, and in favor with God and man." Slowly, calmly, beautifully, that Humanity, which was to be the living temple of Jehovah, grew unto its perfect state. Did Ezekiel in vision behold a stream flowing from under the threshold of the great temple, small at first, but growing ever wider and deeper until it rolled resistlessly on, a mighty river ? So from this other temple, the waters of life have been flowing, scarcely felt at first, flowing gently over men's feet, but growing ever deeper the farther we go with it, now at the ankles, now at the knees, now at the loins, and now flowing over the head.

It would be a long step towards reaching the Truth for which all earnest men are seeking, did we find that "the testimony of Jesus is the Spirit of prophecy." There would then remain but one step more: the glad approach in answer to the "Come unto me." It is feared by some that much of what is reported to have been said and done by the Perfect One is but the embroidery worked upon His vesture by loving friends. We may find, on the other hand, that there are those who still divide His garments among themselves. But as for the "embroidery," we have often thought of the kindly words of personal comfort, so simple that they fairly sweep the ground on which we stand, and the many little deeds of miracle and love in which the truth of this all-gracious Life seemed to terminate, as *the hem of His garment.*

E.

THE SIMPLICITY OF THE GOSPEL RECORDS AND THE MIRACULOUS ELEMENT.

THE Gospels come to us in a form bearing on their face a mark of simple honesty. They are not commentaries. In their letter they are the records of what some plain, true-hearted men saw and heard. That is one of the remarkable evidences of their genuineness, — that they do *not* explain. The facts are given, the sayings of the Saviour, treasured in their memories, are set down without any private interpretation. Take the Transfiguration, for instance. A startling apparition, truly, this sudden beholding of One who but a moment before had stood beside them in all human simplicity, now shining as the sun. And yet the fact alone is recorded, without one word of attempted explanation. Take the Resurrection,— a theme for the study of Christian commentators ever since; and yet one very reason for its credibility is the perfect simplicity and straightforwardness of the record,— not a comment, never a word of apology or attempted explanation, but a plain, brief recital of what was seen and heard. To say that men record their imaginations or preconceptions in a form so terse and historical, is an offence to our common judgment. Besides, the Evangelists record it against themselves more than once, that they who were disciples did not understand many of the things that were said and done until all things had been accomplished, and they could see the full and perfect meaning of their Master's life. They understood not His frequent references to His death and passion; they understood not the "procession of palms"; Peter understood not the foot-washing. But these things were recorded; and the record becomes doubly valuable as showing how little of private interpretation and idiosyncrasy there was in what was written.

And here is a fact which, on the assumption so often made that miracles were an invention of the writers, or misconceptions or exaggerations on the part of credulous beholders, is to say the least strange: *there is no record of a single miracle by the Lord which He performed for Himself.* "He saved others," the people cried exultantly, as they watched Him on the cross; "Himself He cannot save." They mocked Him with His seeming helplessness, and challenged Him to put forth His power and free Himself. "Let Him come down from the cross, and we will believe on Him." And to my mind the strangest miracle in all that holy life is the fact, that throughout all those last scenes of mockery and suffering He never once put forth His power in His own defence; that though they made such cruel sport of Him, though they blindfolded Him, and struck Him, and spit upon Him, though they lashed Him, and dragged Him hither and thither, He would not take Himself out of His tormentors' hands nor do them harm; and that in that last hour, the people reviling, His friends weeping, the pains of death and of hell laying hold of Him, He would not deliver Himself, but just died there between the two thieves. And yet if, as is often maintained, it was inevitable that the life of Christ should have been associated with miracle, how strange it is that not one of the Evangelists should have imagined something miraculous in such scenes as these!

F.

THE STORY OF THE REDEMPTION.

ALL Christians, surely, can unite in a grateful acknowledgment of the new life of thought and love which the Saviour brought into the world. It has been claimed, that for nearly every precept which the Lord taught its equivalent can be found in some older religion; that the Golden Rule, for instance, which the Christ declared to be the very sum and substance of true religion, was taught by Confucius, although in its negative form. But Truth is old; old as Divinity, for it is a part of it. "In the beginning was the Word." And the test of a teacher's or a reformer's greatness is not so much in an ability to discover new truth, as in securing for Truth, whether old or new, its rightful place and power. And this the Lord certainly did. He made truth real, not simply by stating it, however beautifully and clearly, but by *being* it.

Take the law of love, which is declared to be the new commandment of the religion of Jesus. Men had been taught again and again the greatness of love. The fatherless, the stranger, the widow, were commended to the merciful care of every true Israelite. But what had been taught, what had in a variety of ways been imaged and represented, gained an actuality and power through the life of the self-sacrificing love of Jesus of Nazareth which nothing can destroy. Is not the same true of the law of service, of humility, of forbearance, of forgiveness? The Lord has revealed and established these truths as facts, — facts made real and beautiful through the experiences of His divinely human life.

Hence a peculiarity of His teaching, — one

which would be taken as a piece of unbearable egotism if attempted by any one else,— His frequent use of the expression, "*I am.*" What does He say of meekness and lowliness? "*I am* meek and lowly in heart." What does He say of the resurrection and its life? "*I am* the Resurrection and the Life!" There is a way to eternal life: how shall men find it? The Lord's answer is, "*I am* the Way." There is a gate, a means of entrance: but where? And again His answer is, "*I am* the Door." That He would have an influence upon the thought and life of men seemed clear: but how does he express this fact? "*I am* the Vine; ye are the branches." "*I am* the Bread of Life." "*I am* . . . the Truth."

In His teachings, then, in His acts of helpful kindness, in His patient ministry of love, we can see the beginnings of that work of liberation which He had come to accomplish. Men were held by false views of their relation to each other. To them "an eye for an eye, and a tooth for a tooth," expressed the whole idea of justice. Labor was regarded as a curse; poverty a disgrace; death a horror; and the future life a blank. Very quietly, but with a might that has proved triumphant, these forms of bondage were overcome, and to the poor and the sinful doors were opened upon a new life of freedom. As fast as it was possible, men's eyes were opened to see the vileness of evil, and means were provided for their escape. In Him they saw what true life should be. A few were able to be instructed in some of the mysteries of the Kingdom of Heaven. And these the Lord kept about Him. And in order that what He said might be more than a mere matter of learning or of the memory, He let them share some of His work; sent them on little mission tours, that they might have an experience of His own love of doing good. In this way their spiritual power and confidence grew; and when He was removed from their bodily sight, they were helped to believe in His spiritual presence, and went on with their work, strong in the confidence that He would support them in every experience that might befall them.

But there was another side to this great work of redemption, which was for the most part invisible, and yet which was still more important, for it went deeper; still more momentous, for it dealt directly with the sources of evil power. And see; here is a single verse in St. Mark's Gospel that will serve our purpose: "And unclean spirits when they saw Him fell down before Him, and cried, saying, Thou art the Son of God!" Ah, then they knew Him! then in some way they had met Him! had felt the divine power of His life come upon them as a kind of judgment!

"I know Thee who Thou art; the Holy One of God!" Again the same cry! and again it comes from unclean lips! "Thou art the Christ, the Son of God!" Still this same confession from the devil-legion! and always this acknowledgment of a Power they could not face!

The Lord, need it be said, did not treat evil as an outside blemish. It is no mere skin disease. Its roots are deep. It comes from the heart. And what gives it life? What gives hate its unnatural fury? What breath blows upon evil passion until it breaks out into a destroying flame? What is it that gives a fiendish delight to acts of cruelty? Man is a spiritual being. He is created capable of receiving spiritual influences, thinking spiritual thoughts, feeling spiritual affections. Around the souls of infants and little children we love to think there are heavenly influences. Why, we can feel it! And into all good, noble thought, or unselfish service, comes a kind of inspiration and joy which we instinctively speak of as "heavenly." These influences are as real, as necessary to the soul of man, as light and heat of the sun are to the flower. We do not grow from ourselves, but from the assimilation of spiritual forces and substances which we receive into our life. "A man can receive [or, still better, "a man can take unto himself"] nothing except it be given him from heaven," is the strong way in which the Lord states this law of man's receptivity. And not only do little children have angels about them, who, in their holiness, do always behold the face of our Father in heaven, but, on the authority of the Son of Man, "there is joy in the presence of the angels of God over one sinner that repenteth."

And if this law of association between heaven and what is good in man be true, the opposite must also be true. Into evil thoughts, murders, adulteries, fornications, and the like, flow hellish influences, which give them such corrupting power. Was it not so with Judas? In his sordid love of gain, he opened himself to a malign power. That power was not slow in coming. "Then entered Satan into Judas surnamed Iscariot," is the statement of the Gospel. Brief enough, and terrible as brief. Not that Satan, as here and elsewhere mentioned, is some one head devil. That is an old heathen doctrine. "Our name is legion, for we are many," cried the evil spirit at Gadara. And just as we use the word Man as applying to the entire human race, so Satan or Devil is a term covering the entire kingdom of evil spirits. And when it is said that Satan entered into Judas, we understand the statement to mean that into the false, hateful thought of that apostle, into the mean desire to make gain out of One so holy, spirits of evil entered with delight, encouraged his thought, fanned his desire into a flame, until it mastered him, and he did the deed which will always be associated with his name, and which, in the agony of the shame and remorse which succeeded his treachery drove him to self-murder.

In the Lord's day these evil influences were evidently in the ascendency. Little by little man had ceased to make use of those spiritual means and powers by which they can be resisted and withstood. And as a result, man came more and more under the control of this evil dominion. This baleful, infernal influence, which seemed to spread itself between man and heaven, and which threatened to cut off its light and life and leave mankind to stifle and perish in those poisoned atmospheres below, is what is meant by the darkness which would cover the earth, and gross darkness the people. How far that power sometimes went is disclosed to us in the cases of demoniac possession. And those cases, we may believe, were disclosed as a sign of a common danger threatening all humanity, as also to reveal the spiritual nature of the Lord's redeeming work.

For He came face to face with that power; He came into conflict with it. How? The apostle has answered that question: "He was tempted at all points like as we are." The human nature assumed by incarnation, although it lived directly from the Divine, called in the Gospels the Father,—much as a man's body may be said to live from his soul,— was in itself woman-born. It was therefore approachable, not only by men, not only by angels, but by spirits of evil. We frequently read of the Scribes and Pharisees tempting Him, by trying to entrap Him in His speech. Even the unwise affection of Peter, and the hot indignation of the sons of Zebedee, were forms of temptation to turn Him from the way of self-sacrifice and mercy. But what were these as compared with the assaults made upon His human nature by the powers of evil! In every way they tried to find and lay hold of some weakness, some fear, some trace of bitterness, some desire for self-preservation, by which they could gain a foothold, and turn Him from His purpose. At every point, the Apostle declares, they made their attack.

But all in vain. When the mob picked up stones to stone Him, they could bring no fear upon Him. When Peter denied Him, they could not prompt Him to utter a bitter word against the man who rushed out into the night in very shame. When Judas kissed Him, there was no hate; only an exclamation of sad compassion. When false witnesses rose up against Him, there was no word of angry denial or self-vindication. When the cross was lifted, there was no denunciation: only a prayer. When the mob hooted and taunted Him, a silence, as of a pity unutterable, was the only answer. And it troubled them. Somehow the taunts died out as the end drew near. They stood in the gathering darkness in silence. And when it was all over, instead of a cheer, that same rabble at Golgotha were smiting their breasts, and many were saying, "Truly this was the Son of God!"

And if the power of that perfect life would in a few hours affect the mob of Jerusalem so, how would it be with the spirits of evil, who from the first had been met by a power of truth from which they shrank in fear? Can we not see that gradually this power, which kept coming more and more fully into the tempted parts or degrees of His Humanity, would not only be felt by evil spirits, but would awe them, frighten them, scatter them to their own abodes? The Gadarenes begged

Him to depart out of their coasts. There was something about His presence they could not stand. How much more keenly would this be felt by evil beings in the spiritual world. Would not His near presence act upon them as a kind of judgment, and break the unlawful hold which they had gained upon man?

The Lord Himself gives us warrant for such a belief; for He said: "For judgment I am come into this world." "Now is the judgment of this world: now shall the prince of this world be cast out." "I beheld Satan as lightning fall from heaven." The power of evil, which had exalted itself to such a height that the very heavens were threatened, was abased. Back to their own places the spirits of darkness fled; for a Power which they no longer dared to face had conquered them.

And as a result, what? Why, man's spiritual freedom was restored. A new power of life was given. He could turn himself freely either to good or to evil; for redemption is not salvation, but that freedom of spirit which makes salvation possible. And that freedom was universal; it included man everywhere. And being essentially a subjugation of the kingdom of darkness, redemption was just as much for the good of those who never heard the name of the Redeemer, as for those who stood about Him.

A glorious redemption truly! A wonderful deliverance from a monstrous tyranny. Man may indeed be subject to evil influences from within. But this is largely because he invites and indulges them. And even then, if he will but turn to the Lord the Redeemer, there is no limit to the power which he may call to his aid, save the limit of his own power of reception.

And this certainly is what we can see to-day:

a growing freedom of thought, a newness of life, a new power of affection, which are gradually transforming our existence. And all this in its very first and most immediate cause is traceable, not to any great school of philosophy, not to any royal court nor patron, but to this Life that was first seen in far-off Galilee, and that quietly taught on sea-shore and mountain.

There is but one Life that is so felt. If He were mere man, it would not be so. Nor could we rest in Him; for no purely human being can be the final refuge of those who seek God. But men do rest in the Christ; men do feel His spirit. The Gospels tell of Him, the Church witnesses Him, but the human heart alone feels Him. And what is this if not a fulfilment of His last pledge made to men on the earth, "Lo, I am with you always!"

✠

"Nor can the vain toil cease
Till in the shadowy maze of life we meet
One who can guide our aching, wayward feet
To find Himself, — our Way, our Life, our Peace.
In Him the long unrest is soothed and stilled,
Our hearts are filled."

✠

www.ingramcontent.com/pod-product-compliance
Lightning Source LLC
Chambersburg PA
CBHW020909230426
43666CB00008B/1373